KICKBOXING
TRAINING DRILLS

KICKBOXING TRAINING DRILLS

Justyn Billingham

THE CROWOOD PRESS

First published in 2011 by
The Crowood Press Ltd
Ramsbury, Marlborough
Wiltshire SN8 2HR

www.crowood.com

British Library Cataloguing-in-Publication Data
A catalogue record for this book is available from the British Library.

ISBN 978 1 84797 287 3

Disclaimer
Please note that the author and the publisher of this book are not
responsible in any manner whatsoever for any damage or injury of any
kind that may result from practising, or applying, the principles, ideas,
techniques and/or following the instructions/information described in
this publication. Since the physical activities described in this book may
be too strenuous in nature for some readers to engage in safely, it is
essential that a doctor be consulted before undertaking training.

Typeset by Jean Cussons Typesetting, Diss, Norfolk

Printed and bound in Malaysia by Times Offset (M) Sdn Bhd

Contents

Dedication

I would like to dedicate this book to all my students, past and present. It's you who have made this book possible.

Acknowledgements

Thanks to my good friend Nigel, for 'bullying' me into writing this, my third book. I'm glad you did. Thanks to Katie and Sarah for giving up their time to appear in yet another book. Thanks to my wife Sam for taking all the photos, and for all her help and support as always, and thanks also to Harley and Izzy, my two beautiful children, for putting up with being dragged to more photo shoots and never complaining. I couldn't have done it without your support.

Foreword

Wow, here you have yourself a new book – make sure you use it wisely. Justyn's passion and the way he structures the knowledge he has will equip you with a great set of skills. I am honoured to introduce his latest work to you, as I know that Justyn is very diligent and precise in his teachings and he continues to learn, study and rediscover his martial arts and make it *his* life's work.

Life for me would be empty without a space filled with martial arts. The study of the arts is an unbelievable journey of self-discovery. The voyage will uncover aspects of yourself that you never knew existed. Strength, courage, honour and mental tenacity, to name just a few. Whether you choose simply to dip your toes into the martial-arts pool of knowledge, or jump head first and immerse yourself in its vast ocean, there's a place for you. You don't have to become a lifelong student of the game; you can simply be a casual observer, or just sit somewhere in-between (maybe even somewhere beyond if that is your choosing).

Justyn's work will help you on your path to wherever you happen to be travelling. Just one technique learned and applied from this book will be worth the money you spent on it. I know that the training drills on these pages have been selected, with many hours spent compiling a seamless transition of information, in order to give the reader the best vantage point they can have.

Blend what you learn from Justyn and make it useful to your game and your art, but don't stop there. Keep searching for new ways to improve your level and enjoy your pursuit; the time and labour you put in will be returned back to you in many ways. To say I owe a lot to the martial arts would be an understatement. I owe my life to the study of the martial arts, as it's made me who I am today.

Have fun, train hard, breathe it, become it and 'it' will become you.

Peace,

David Lee

Combat Submission Wrestling/MMA Instructor under Erik Paulson
Brazilian Jiu Jitsu Brown Belt under Ze Marcello
Bushido Challenge Featherweight Champion
Ultimate Challenge Featherweight Champion
6 × Cage Rage veteran
2 × UFC (Ultimate Fighting Champion) veteran

Introduction

To the uninitiated, a kick is a kick and a punch is a punch. To the experienced martial artist, however, it is so much more. You see, a punch (or kick) is actually made up of a series of elements that all come together at exactly the right moment to make the punch (or kick) as effective as it can be. Those elements include such things as speed, power, targeting, technique and timing. On top of these, you need to add in movement, footwork, energy, fitness, defences and, most importantly of all, belief. You could easily have the fastest kicks, the most powerful punch, incredible agility and lightning-fast speed, but these are of no use to you if you don't believe you are good enough. I remember a wise old instructor I once had the honour of training with tell me that he had seen many a great warrior (*top level martial artist*) fall in battle (*get beaten in a street fight*) because their mind was that of a baby (*they hadn't focused enough on the mental aspect of their training to truly believe in their ability*).

Having spent the best part of my life studying martial arts and developing my kicking and punching ability to a level I would consider to be (slightly) above average, it became apparent to me that just knowing what a punch or kick should look like was simply not enough. For some that's all that is needed, but, being the analytical kind of person that I am, I needed to know exactly what made a punch or kick successful and how I could use my knowledge to make my technical ability as good as it could be.

Through my study and training of several different fighting arts over many years, I believe I found my answers. From then on it seemed only logical that a book detailing how to develop the punch (or kick) should be written. As such, and through my years of training and research, this book aims to break down all of the elements we naturally use (or should be using) when we, as practising martial artists (or sport martial artists), execute our punching, kicking and fighting ability.

This book will show you how to develop these elements using simple-to-follow training drills that you can work on your own, with a partner, or in a class environment (for those of you teaching classes). What this book won't show you, however, is how to execute each technique. It is assumed that you should already know how to do this. Instead, this book will show you how to take the techniques you already use and, by isolating and developing the individual core elements found hidden within each technique, turn your basic kick or punch into a devastating or even world-class kick or punch – providing, of course, that you believe you can do it.

And if at this stage you don't believe you can do it, simply turn to the final chapter of this book and I'll teach you that as well …

Equipment List

Items of training equipment that you might want to consider buying (if you do not already own them) to assist you with using this book are:

- ankle weights
- bag gloves
- blockers
- break board(s) and holder
- coaching mitts
- countdown timer
- focus pads
- hand wraps
- heart-rate monitor
- kick shield
- large clock with second hand

Training Times/Repetitions

Training for Time	*Training for Repetitions*
Beginner level: 30–60 seconds	Beginner level: 10 reps
Intermediate level: 60–90 seconds	Intermediate level: 10–20 reps
Advanced level: 90–120 seconds	Advanced level: 20–35 reps

- maize ball
- punch bag
- resistance band
- stopwatch
- string or thin rope
- Swiss ball
- Thai pads
- weighted vest
- weighted gloves

Training Times/Repetitions

All the training drills contained in this section can either be done for a set period of time or a set number of repetitions. As a rough guide, my suggestion would be to work them (as above).

Rest Periods

You can govern your rest periods in one of two different ways. Initially, they can be based on a simple time duration that can be varied according to your current level of fitness. For example, as a beginner you could rest somewhere between 90sec to 2min, whereas an advanced student should be resting for no longer then 60sec.

Alternatively, you can use a heart-rate monitor and commence the next round once your heart rate decreases to a certain level. Use the table below as a rough guide in order to get you started. You'll notice that when using a heart-rate monitor the rest period remains the same for all levels. This is because the heart rate of an advanced student is likely to reduce down to 120 beats per minute (bpm) much more quickly than the heart rate of someone new to physical exercise. As a result of this and regardless of your current fitness level, the time it takes for your heart rate to return to 120bpm is generally regarded as an acceptable time frame of rest before commencing the next training drill.

Rest Periods

Rest Period in Seconds	*Rest Period Using Heart Rate*
Beginner level: 120–90sec	Beginner level: 120bpm
Intermediate level: 90–60sec	Intermediate level: 120bpm
Advanced level: 60–30sec	Advanced level: 120bpm

1 Warm-Up Drills

The warm-up is probably the most important training drill for the sportsperson, as it prepares the body for the exercise about to be undertaken. I know of many 'rookie' athletes (mainly joggers) who 'don't have the time and/or patience' to warm up properly before going on a run and instead start out at a pace they should only really be hitting at least 20min into their training. I was guilty of this at times, especially in my younger days, when I was arrogant, impatient and too keen to get the boxing gloves on and start sparring instead of easing my body into it gently. Bizarrely, I would find myself 'hitting the wall' a lot sooner than I did when training in a class (where we warmed up properly).

The reason I would hit the wall a lot sooner when training in this way was revealed to me years later while flicking through one of the many health and fitness magazines that grace the shelves. In this day and age, it would be hard not to know about the risks involved in pulling muscles, straining joints, tearing ligaments and so on when we don't warm up properly. Imagine starting a car on a cold morning, then racing off at 100 miles an hour. Even without the technical knowledge of an F1 mechanic, we know that eventually something is going to go 'bang'.

What I didn't realize in my youth is that when the human body goes from cold to 100 per cent, it acts in a similar way to how it does when we enter 'fight or flight mode' (the natural response to a dangerous situation). We receive a huge dump of adrenaline, the heart starts racing faster to get blood to the muscles and the whole body goes into overdrive. While the body doesn't enter full fight or flight mode, as there's no danger element, when you go from nothing to full-on training you experience similar chemical reactions. As the body can't sustain an increased workload of this extent for more than about 30sec (if you don't train for fight or flight), we experience 'burn-out' a lot quicker. Try racing up a set of stairs from cold and see what happens.

So, not only is the warm-up a crucial part of your training, but if you don't warm the body up properly, you will find that you hit the wall a lot quicker than you normally would. For that reason, the following set of warm-up drills will help to prepare the body for exercise, activating all the core elements in the correct way (for the martial artist) and ensuring that you can move on to the other training drills in the book confident in the knowledge of having done all you can to greatly reduce the risk of injury while training.

Warm-Up Drill 1

Skipping

Skipping is a great exercise for warming up as it activates a large number of muscle groups, starts the heart beating faster and is relatively low-

---

Choosing a Skipping Rope

Choose your rope wisely and ensure it is the correct size for you. If you stand in the middle of the rope, the handles should reach up to your armpits. If it is any shorter, it won't pass over your head properly. If it is any longer, you can tie a knot in each side (close to the handles) to help reduce the length. There are also many different types of rope available. My personal preference is the nylon type as it is not too heavy but great for speed skipping. Try a few until you get one you are comfortable with.

---

impact. There are many different ways to skip, however. To begin with, simply bounce from foot to foot, keeping up on the balls of your feet at all times. Try jumping only slightly so that the rope just passes under your feet. Set your timer for 5min and away you go (Fig. 1).

Warm-Up Drill 2

Upper Body Rotations

After skipping we will begin loosening off the joints and starting the synovial fluid flowing, which will help to lubricate the joints in preparation for the next stage of your training.

In a relaxed stance, turn your head to the left (Fig. 2). Roll it very slowly down to your chest (Fig. 3), then across to the other side (Fig. 4). From here, roll it back in the opposite direction. Be careful not to roll the head in a complete circle, however. Where the neck is concerned it's far better to isolate the forward direction and then isolate the backward direction.

Do this ten times, rolling the head forward and then ten times rolling the head backward.

Then start circling the arms forward for ten revolutions (Figs 5–8).

Fig. 1   Skipping.

Fig. 2   Roll the neck to the left.

Fig. 3   … to the centre.

Fig. 4   … to the right.

Fig. 5   Take the arms up.

Fig. 6   Arms forward.

Fig. 7   Arms down.

Fig. 8   Back to the top.

Fig. 9   Arms out to the side.

Fig. 10   Arms across the body.

Fig. 11   Roll the hips clockwise.

Fig. 12   Roll the hips anti-clockwise.

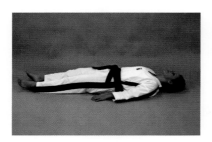

Fig. 13 Lie on your back.

Fig. 14 Raise the leg up.

Fig. 15 Lie on your side.

Fig. 16 Raise the outer leg up.

And then take them backward for ten revolutions. Finally, swing the arms across the body ten times (Figs 9 and 10).

Warm-Up Drill 3

Lower Body Rotations

From here, we'll move on to the lower body rotations. With feet in a shoulder-width stance, rotate your hips in a clockwise direction ten times. Follow this with rotations in an anti-clockwise direction ten more times (Figs 11 and 12).

Lie on your back (Fig. 13) and slowly raise your left leg up to a 90-degree angle (Fig. 14), before slowly lowering down again. Do this ten times with the left leg, then repeat the exercise with the right leg.

Lie on your left side (Fig. 15) and slowly raise your right leg up as high as you can (Fig. 16), before bringing it back down again using the same speed. Repeat this ten times with the right leg, before switching sides and repeating the exercise again with the left leg.

This time, position yourself on all fours as shown in Fig. 17, then raise your left leg up into a cocked position (Fig. 18). Circle the leg forward ten times, then circle the leg backward ten times. Repeat with the right leg (Figs 19–21).

Finally, keeping yourself in the same position as you were in for the last drill, raise your left leg out behind you as high as you can before lowering it slowly back in toward your chest. Repeat this exercise ten times and then switch legs (Figs 22–24).

Once you have completed this final drill, repeat drills 1–3 once more, exactly as described above. This should ensure your joints are mobilized and fully lubricated before moving on to the next set of warm-up drills.

Warm-Up Drill 4

Lower Body Warm-Up

This next section of warm-up drills will start the heart pumping faster, get the muscles working

Fig. 17   On all fours.

Fig. 18   Raise the leg up.

Fig. 19   Rotate the leg forward …

Fig. 20   … toward the floor.

Fig. 21   … back round to the start.

Fig. 22   On all fours.

Fig. 23   Extend the leg back.

Fig. 24   Drive the knee forward.

Fig. 25   Jogging on the spot.

Fig. 26   Flick your heels behind you.

Fig. 27   Jogging on the spot.

Fig. 28   Raise your knees high.

Fig. 29   From an upright position.

Fig. 30   Squat down.

harder and start raising your overall core body temperature, which are all essential elements for injury-free training.

Start jogging on the spot, staying on the balls of the feet and flicking your heels up behind you as high as they will go (Figs 25 and 26). This can also be done while jogging around a room, running track or playing field. You can do this in one of two ways:

• either jog for a set time period (somewhere between 30 and 60sec is as an ideal starting point)

• or jog for a set number of repetitions. Somewhere between 30 and 75sec should be enough (each time your left foot comes off the floor count one, two, three and so on).

This time as you jog, bring your knees up as high as you can – aim to bring your knees up to your waist at the very least. Follow the same guidelines as above for length and duration (Figs 27 and 28).

Once the legs have been warmed up sufficiently, introduce a muscle-activating exercise, such as squats. The squat is an excellent exercise for building strength in the legs, but just be aware that's not what we are aiming to achieve at this point. Instead, we need to warm the legs up just enough so that when we commence kicking, the muscles have already started working and there's less risk of injury. You will also notice a huge difference in your kicking if you first warm the legs up in this way. My suggestion would be to perform no more then ten squats at this stage.

From an upright position, place your fingers on your temples (Fig. 29) and lower your body down by bending your knees so that you touch your elbows and knees together, being careful not to bend your back (Fig. 30).

The final exercise we can introduce to warm up the legs is the simple lunge. From an upright position (Fig. 31), step forward with your left leg as shown in Fig. 32. As you step, be sure to not bring the knee further forward than the lead foot. In one motion, step back to the upright position, then step forward again with the other leg. Repeat this exercise ten times with each leg (so twenty times in total), before moving on to the next exercise.

Warm-Up Drill 5

Total Body Warm-Up

For the final stage of the warm-up, we are going to finish with some total body warm-up drills. This ensures that the body is warm, the joints have been loosened off and you are ready for the next stage of your training.

From a standing position with slightly bent legs (Fig. 33), jump out with both feet, bringing your arms above your head at the same time as you land (Fig. 34). From this position, jump straight back to the starting position without pausing. This is one repetition.

Fig. 31 From standing.

Fig. 32 Lunge forward with your lead leg.

BELOW LEFT: Fig. 33 From an upright position.

BELOW RIGHT: Fig. 34 Perform a star jump.

Repeat each move ten times so that you perform ten Star Jumps without pausing in-between. If you're not familiar with the Star Jump (or Jumping Jacks as they're also known), it might take a few practice jumps to get used to the movement. The key to the success of this exercise is evenly paced jumps, staying light on the balls of your feet throughout.

The final total body warm-up exercise that we'll incorporate is, in my opinion, the best one – the burpee. From a standing position (Fig. 35),

drop into a squat (Fig. 36). Kick the legs out fully (Fig. 37) before bringing them back to a squat position (Fig. 38). From here, jump into the air as high as you can, powering up through the legs (Fig. 39). Ten of these are probably all you need at this stage as we're still warming the body up and anything you do that is too hard or too rigorous at this stage will only aid in tiring the muscles, which will be counterproductive to your actual training.

Fig. 35   From standing.

Fig. 36   Squat down ...

Fig. 37   ... kick the legs back.

Fig. 38   ... return to the squat.

Fig. 39   ... jump into the air.

2 Stretching Drills

The next stage in your training is stretching. Stretching is a key element in any form of physical exercise, especially for the kickboxer. In order to develop your kicking ability, it is first necessary to develop your flexibility. If you don't, the lack of movement in the legs and hips will prevent you kicking to your true potential. A lack of kicking ability will seriously hinder the development of the muscles that are employed when kicking, with the result that you will always be kicking below your potential maximum level.

When I perform stretching exercises, I like to focus on a full body stretch working from the head right down to the legs. For the upper body, I follow a simple basic stretching programme that takes the joints through their full range of movement (that is, a greater amount of movement than they would go through in normal use). However, the focus of the lower body stretching is to increase the range of movement in the joints for this area, allowing the hips to open further and the legs to move in a greater range than they are otherwise designed to do for normal, everyday living.

Stretching Drill 1

Upper Body Stretching

Place your left hand onto the right side of your

Fig. 40   Gently stretch the neck to the side.

Fig. 41   Gently stretch the neck forward.

Fig. 42   Gently stretch the neck backward.

Fig. 43   Stretch the arm across the body.

head and very gently pull your head across to the opposite side (Fig. 40). As you perform this stretch, try not actually to pull the head to the side, but instead simply rest the hand on the head and let the weight of the hand do all the work. Hold this stretch for a count of 10sec, then repeat the exercise on the other side.

From here, place the hands on the back of your head and gently pull your head forward (Fig. 41). Use the same rule of force as above, again holing the stretch for a count of 10sec.

Finally, place your fingers lightly on your forehead and gently push your head backward (Fig. 42). You will find that it helps if you keep your mouth open while performing this stretch. Hold the stretch for a count of 10sec as before.

Now take your right arm across your body and by curling your left arm around it, pull it in to your body as tightly as you can (Fig. 43). You should feel the stretch on your shoulder for this one. Hold for a count of 10sec and then repeat the stretch using the other arm.

From here use your arm to reach down your back as far as you can and assist the stretch fur-

ther by pushing down on your elbow with your other hand (Fig. 44). Hold the stretch for a count of 10sec, then repeat the exercise on the other side.

Standing in a shoulder-width stance, point your right hand up toward the ceiling, then take it over your head while leaning to the left side (Fig. 45). This exercise will stretch out the side (oblique) muscles. Hold the stretch for a count of 10sec.

Stretching With Caution

As with all the stretches, exercise caution while moving in and out of the position, particularly when performing stretches that start to engage the back. One overenthusiastic movement is all that is needed to put your back out and keep you from training for many months. Very slow and deliberate movements are all that you should be doing when performing any type of stretching exercise, particularly the next few sets of stretches.

Fig. 44   Stretch the arm down the back.

Fig. 45   Bend to the side.

Fig. 46   Drop the body forward.

Now we are going to focus on stretching out the back. We do this by rolling the spine forward one vertebrae at a time. Try to image curling into a ball instead of simply leaning forward. By leaning we increase the workload on the lower back, which may not be strong enough to support the weight of the torso (especially if it's a large torso!). This is extremely important – therefore it is essential that you don't get it wrong.

Once in position, simply relax the upper body, focusing in particular on relaxing the head, shoulders, arms and back. To help with this, don't think of it as a stretching exercise, but rather as more of a 'hang'. Hang for a count of 10sec before raising yourself up slowly and carefully (Fig. 46).

Finally, and to counterbalance the previous movement, place your hands on your waist and push your hips forward as you lean backward at the same time. If done correctly, you'll feel this stretch on your abdominal (stomach) muscles. Your objective with this stretch is to look at the

Fig. 47   Push the hips forward.

Fig. 48   Stretch the quadriceps.

Fig. 49   Touch your toes.

wall behind you, although realistically you probably won't achieve this unless you are double-jointed or have an incredibly supple back. Keeping your mouth open once again as you perform this stretch will help a great deal. Hold for 10sec before returning to an upright position slowly and carefully (Fig. 47).

Stretching Drill 2

Lower Body Stretching

That final upper body stretch takes us nicely into the lower body stretching. The focus here is to enhance your level of flexibility in order to increase the overall movement of the joints in preparation for the kicks.

From a standing position, take hold of your shin (there is a risk of hyperextending the joint if you take hold of your foot, so try to avoid this area) and pull the leg up toward the rear of your body. As you do this, gently push the hip forward and you'll feel the stretch increase (Fig. 48). If you have trouble with your balance at this stage, it's totally acceptable to support yourself with

your other hand. You can also try focusing on a spot on the floor or wall in front of you and holding your spare arm out to the side for balance. Hold the stretch for a count of 10sec and repeat using the other leg.

Now place your feet together and roll your body forward (remember not to lean forward with this kind of stretch), reaching as far down your legs as you can (Fig. 49). If you can, touch your toes, then try touching the floor. If you can touch the floor, try placing your hands flat on the floor. Once you are in your lowest position, hold the stretch for a count of 10sec.

Now grab the backs of your legs as far down as you can. From this position, pull your chest closer to your legs and hold the stretch for a further count of 10sec (Fig. 50).

Now take a seat on the floor. Place your left leg out in front of you and tuck your right leg into the body as shown. Grab your left leg at the lowest point you can and gently pull your chest down toward your knee (Fig. 51). Hold the stretch for a count of 10sec, then repeat the stretch with your other leg.

Fig. 50   Pull yourself closer.

Fig. 51   Pull your chest down to your leg.

Fig. 52   Pull your chest down to both legs.

Fig. 53   The butterfly stretch.

Now place both legs out in front of you and slide your hands underneath your legs, as far down as you can. Placing the hands underneath the legs in this way gives you slightly more leverage than simply taking hold of them in the traditional way. From here, pull the chest down to both legs this time and hold the stretch for a count of 10sec (Fig. 52).

Now bring your feet together and pull them in as close to the body as you can. By taking hold of the feet or ankles and resting your elbows on your thighs, you can push down with your legs, aided by further pushing with your elbows, and drive the legs as close to the floor as you can get them (Fig. 53). Hold the stretch for a count of 10sec.

From here, go into a squat position and stretch your left leg out toward the side wall so that it rests on the heel with your toes pointing up toward the ceiling. Bend your rear leg and bring your foot up on to the ball, keeping your heel off the floor. Push your rear knee out with your right

21

Fig. 54   Extend the leg out to the side.

Fig. 55   Keep the foot flat on the floor.

Fig. 56   Drop the body to the centre.

Fig. 57   Pull the body down to the leg.

elbow and hold the stretch at your lowest position for a count of 10sec (Fig. 54). Repeat the stretch with your other leg.

Continue as you did for the previous stretch, except this time change the stretch slightly so that both feet now remain flat on the floor (Fig. 55). Hold for a further count of 10sec.

From here, lock the legs out straight into a double shoulder-width stance and lower your body down toward the floor. Hold the stretch as low as you can for a count of 10sec (Fig. 56).

Then reach across to your left leg and by taking hold of your ankle (or the lowest point you can reach), pull your head and chest down to your left leg (Fig. 57). Hold for a count of 10sec, then repeat the stretch on the other side.

Finally, take a seat on the floor and stretch your legs out as wide as possible (Fig. 58). From here, bring your body down to the centre, aiming to get your chest as close to the ground as possible (Figs 59 and 60). Hold the stretch at your lowest position for a count of 10sec.

For the upper body, you will only need to perform each stretch once. However, as we are aiming to increase the range of movement in the joints with the lower body stretching drills, my suggestion is to perform each of the lower body stretching drills a total of three times. For example, you would work through all of the lower body stretches, from Fig. 48 to Fig. 60. Then start back at Fig. 48 and work them through to Fig. 60 for a second time, before repeating for a third and final time.

If you do this properly, as outlined above, and remove the temptation to rush through the drills or even miss some out, you will find that by the third and final stretch your legs are not only fully warmed up, but the range of movement between the first set of stretches and the third set will be greatly increased.

Fig. 58   Sit with your legs wide.

Fig. 59   Bring your elbows to the floor.

Fig. 60   Bring your chest to the floor.

3 Developing the Basics

As mentioned in the introduction, this book isn't going to show you what each technique is or how to perform it, as it is assumed you already possess this knowledge. If you don't, or if you need more training on the basic kicks and punches found in kickboxing, you might want to consider buying my first book, *Kickboxing from Beginner to Black Belt* (The Crowood Press 2008), before moving on. However, to avoid any confusion as to what techniques you will be using in this book, I've detailed the most popular ones in this short chapter, with brief explanations on the way each technique works.

The Basic Hand Techniques

The Jab
A fast-moving set-up punch that is used to probe through or break down a guard and assist in the set-up of a knockout technique. It is not generally considered to be a knockout technique in itself and is always thrown from the lead hand (Fig. 61).

The Cross
A powerful back-hand punch that is capable of delivering knockout power. It is generally used as part of a combination of punches and is most commonly associated with the jab (Fig. 62).

Fig. 61   The jab.

Fig. 62   The cross.

Fig. 63   The lead hook.

Fig. 64   The rear hook.

The Lead Hook

A circular punch very much associated with the knockout. The lead hook is an incredibly fast punch that can be used just as effectively in attack as in defence. The main targeting area of the lead hook is the chin or temple (Fig. 63).

The Rear Hook

As with the cross, this punch can deliver knock-out power from the rear hand and works best when used as part of a combination of punches. Don't overlook the effectiveness of the rear hook when used to attack the body of an opponent (Fig. 64).

The Lead Uppercut

A rising punch designed to attack the underside of the chin, the solar plexus or the floating ribs. Due to the way this punch travels it is an incredibly effective close-range technique and is great at finding a way through the bottom of an open guard (Fig. 65).

Fig. 65   The lead uppercut.

The Rear Uppercut

The rear uppercut is the final punch in a kick-boxer's arsenal. As with all rear-hand punches it is incredibly powerful, albeit a bit slow compared to its lead-hand counterpart. The advantage of the uppercut is that it can be thrown from angles that other punches can't and as such it's an incredibly effective counter-punch and more than capable of stopping a fight (Fig. 66).

The Backfist Strike

Possibly the fastest of all the hand techniques, the backfist strike is an incredible set-up technique that can be used as an attacking or counter-attacking technique, as will be seen later in the book. The principle of the backfist strike is the same as the jab, although it is used to attack at a different angle (Fig. 67).

The Lead Elbow

Although not strictly a hand technique, these last two weapons are used in a great many fighting

Fig. 66   The rear uppercut.

Fig. 67   The backfist strike.

Fig. 68   The lead elbow.

arts, so are worth including in this section. Used primarily for close-range fighting, the sheer nature of the elbow strike in attack is one of total devastation and as such certain styles of elbow strike have been banned from use in competition (Fig. 68).

The Rear Elbow
As above, only a lot more powerful (Fig. 69).

The Basic Kicking Techniques

The Lead Front Kick
A forward-facing straight leg kick that derives its power from the hips. This kick is not only very powerful, but is also very effective. It is a kick you will find yourself using time and time again, hence its inclusion here (Fig. 70).

The Rear Leg Front Kick
This alternate version of the preceding kick is thrown from the rear leg and as with all rear leg kicks is very powerful (Fig. 71).

Fig. 69   The rear elbow.

Fig. 70   The lead front kick.

Fig. 71   The rear front kick.

The Lead Leg Round Kick

Probably one of the most versatile of kicks. The round kick can attack any height with equal effect and can be thrown from almost all positions. It is a popular kick with the full-contact fighters and is probably the kick you will use above all others (Fig. 72). There is no photograph showing the rear round kick as the images would look the same.

The Lead Leg Side Kick

One of few kicks that work equally as well in attack as in defence. The side kick is a straight leg kick that is generally thrown from a side-on stance. From experience, it works most effectively when used to attack the body. However, it can be used to attack both high and low areas (Fig. 73).

Lead and Rear Techniques

The general rule regarding lead and rear techniques is that anything thrown off the lead is generally done for speed, or to set up a knock-out attack (although this does not necessarily mean it lacks knockout power) and anything thrown off the rear is generally done for power.

The Axe Kick

Now we start to focus on more of the advanced kicking techniques, with an incredibly effective kick in the hands of a skilled kicker. The axe kick travels straight up toward the ceiling and back

Fig. 72 The round kick.

Fig. 73 The side kick

Fig. 74　The start of the axe kick.

Fig. 75　The axe kick.

down toward the floor, using dynamic movement to generate the power. As you can see, it is most effective when thrown across the body and usually targets the blind side (the lead side) of an opponent (Figs 74 and 75).

The Hooking Kick

The hooking kick is a slight variation on the side kick. It is thrown toward the side of an opponent and then driven in toward the target using a whipping motion that is generated from the knee joint. It is a very effective kick that can be used to attack around the back of the guard (Figs 76 and 77).

The Spinning Back Kick

Although referred to as a spinning kick, this kick is actually more of a twisting kick, as a spin would cause you to miss your target. The kick is thrown from the rear leg using the twisting motion to generate the power. This is probably the most powerful kick you will ever use (Figs 78 to 80).

Fig. 76　The start of the hooking kick.

29

Fig. 77   The hooking kick.

Fig. 78   Spinning back kick start position.

Fig. 79   Turn the back.

Fig. 80   The spinning back kick.

The Spinning Hook Kick

This is one of the most effective spinning kicks, hence its inclusion here. The spinning hook kick needs an in-depth understanding of speed and timing in order to land it, but, with practice, it can be one of the most formidable weapons in your kicking arsenal (Figs 81 to 84).

Fig. 81   Spinning hook kick start position.

Fig. 82   Turn your back.

Fig. 83   The spin.

Fig. 84   The spinning hook kick.

4 Developing Power

People often confuse power with strength, but when referring to power in relation to martial arts (or kickboxing) it is a totally different thing. We often associate strength with lifting, pulling or pushing and more commonly with regard to weight training or similar sporting activities that require their participants to have particular strength in relation to the activity performed.

Strength certainly plays its part in the martial arts. However, we tend to find that technique often outperforms strength in respect of punching and kicking. Evidence of this can be clearly seen in the many reality-based mixed martial-arts style competitions that have become very popular just recently when the lighter, smaller, more wiry combatant beats the muscle-bound giant in a David versus Goliath style match up (just watch the early episodes of Ultimate Fighting Championships to see what I am talking about). Often a fighter is referred to as having 'knockout power' and rarely, if at all, referred to as having 'knockout strength'. 'Strength' and 'power' have different dictionary descriptions and must be regarded as separate elements.

As power is a key element in a successful punch or kick, this chapter will provide you with isolated training drills to help you to develop fully this element and ensure your kicks and punches carry knockout power with them.

IMPORTANT – Ensure that you have warmed up and stretched correctly before moving on to the following training drills. Use the training guides at the start of the book to assist you.

Training Drill 1

The Jumping Lunge
This simple training drill helps you to develop explosive power in the legs. Having powerful legs

Fig. 85   Jumping lunges.

Fig. 86   The jump.

Fig. 87   The switch.

not only enhances your kicking ability but also helps to delay the onset of muscle fatigue in this area, particularly when using your footwork to move around.

Starting off with your left leg forward (Fig. 85), jump as high as you can into the air (Fig. 86) switching legs and landing back into a lunge position with the opposite leg forward (Fig. 87). Immediately spring back up and switch the legs back. When performing a lunge make sure the lead knee does not extend past the toes.

Training Drill 2

The Push-Up

The push-up is a great exercise for developing power in the upper body (Figs 88 and 89). You can work a push-up in several different ways in order to develop different muscle groups. For punching and developing your guard position, I would recommend the close-arm push-up as shown in Fig. 92.

In the table below is a brief description of the main areas that each style of push-up helps to develop.

The more advanced push-up drills such as the one-arm medicine ball push-up and the Swiss ball push-up can also be varied using different hand positions to work different muscle groups, such as the upper chest muscles, for example.

My suggestion for these exercises would be to add variety to your workouts by doing a different style of push-up each time, starting off with the wide-arm push-up, for example, and working through to the Swiss ball push-ups. Alternatively, you could choose to take several (I would suggest no more than three) of the push-up drills below and use those as part of an overall upper body power development training programme.

Fig. 88 Push-up start position.

Fig. 89 Push-up finish position.

Push-Ups

Exercise	Development
Wide-arm push-up (Fig. 90)	Power in the chest
Standard push-up (Fig. 91)	Power in the chest and triceps
Close-arm push-up (Fig. 92)	Power in the triceps
One-arm push-up (Fig. 93)	Isolating muscle groups
Clapping push-up (Figs 94–96)	Explosive power
One-arm medicine ball push-up (Figs 97–100)	Power and endurance
Medicine ball push-up (Figs 101–102)	Power and stabilizing
Swiss ball push-up (Figs 103–104)	Power in the upper chest area

Fig. 90   Wide-arm push-up.

Fig. 91   Standard push-up.

Fig. 92   Close-arm push-up.

Fig. 93   One-arm push-up.

Fig. 94   Clapping push-ups start position.

Fig. 95   Drop the body down.

Fig. 96   Push-up and clap.

Fig. 97   Medicine ball push-up.

Fig. 98   Perform a push-up.

Fig. 99   Jump across to the other side.

Fig. 100   Perform a push-up.

Fig. 101   Close arm-ups on a medicine ball.

Fig. 102   Finish position.

Fig. 103   Swiss ball push-up.

Fig. 104   Finish position.

Training Drill 3

The Sit-Up

Sit-ups are great for developing a powerful core. The core is basically the stabilizing muscles that support the body structure. A well-developed core will support you even better, as well as offering additional protection to the internal organs, particularly from blows to the midsection.

There are many ways to develop this area using basic exercises such as standard sit-ups and crunches and as good as these are, I have also included some additional ones to give you some variety on these popular training drills.

Weighted Crunch

Wearing a weighted vest (Fig. 105), perform a crunch by bringing the knees and elbows together and holding for a second before relaxing and repeating the movement (Figs 106 and 107).

Alternatively, if you don't have access to a weighted vest, you can try holding a weight plate against the chest as shown in Fig. 108.

Fig. 105   The weighted vest.

Fig. 106   Weighted vest sit-ups.

Fig. 107   Hold at the top.

Fig. 108   Weight plate sit-up.

Fig. 109   Swiss ball sit-up.

Fig. 110   Hold at the top.

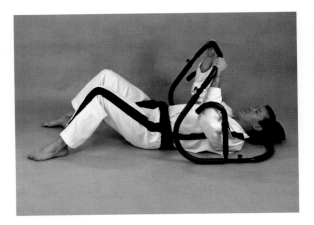

Fig. 111   Using equipment to train with.

Fig. 112   The sit-up.

Swiss Ball Sit-Up

Position yourself on a Swiss ball so that you are sitting nearer the front of the ball and using your legs to balance you. Keep your fingers on your temples and lower the body backward as far as you can comfortably go. When you reach the lowest point, raise back up to the start position using your abdominal muscles only. Hold for a second and repeat (Figs 109 and 110).

Ab Cruncher

Another excellent training aid to help develop a powerful core is an ab cruncher (you may know it by a different name as there are many on the market). The ab cruncher is designed to keep your form and movement exactly right as you transition through the various stages of the sit-up. These devices were very popular when they first came out, but, despite most people owning one at some point, the popularity soon wore off as people failed to develop the promised six-packs (generally due to a lack of understanding regarding diet).

If you have one in storage somewhere, blow the dust off it and start using it again as it will help to develop your core like no other device on the market (Figs 111 and 112).

Fig. 113   Partner-assisted sit-up.

Fig. 114   Add in the jab.

Fig. 115   Add in the cross.

Partner-Assisted Sit-Up

There are many things a partner can do to assist you when performing sit-ups however this training drill will help you to develop several areas at the same time. Initially the sit-up movement helps to develop the core and by combining it with a jab, cross combination at the top, you also help to develop power in the oblique (side) muscles due to the twisting motion when punching. Furthermore, it helps to develop power in your punches by isolating the upper body due to the fact that the legs have now been removed from the equation.

As you will realize from this drill, the legs and hips are used a lot when punching while standing and you will notice the difference immediately once they are taken away (Figs 113 to 115).

Training Drill 4

50 Per Cent Power Drill

The principle behind this drill is to remove 50 per cent of the power from the initial techniques and then slowly build up to 100 per cent. For example, in round one you hit the pads in one of three ways:

- isolated technique (such as a jab only)
- set techniques (such as hands only, legs only, straight techniques only, or circular techniques only)
- any technique (such as hands and legs based on how the pads are held).

As you hit the pads, you reduce the power of each attack by 50 per cent. You then rest for a set period of time (refer to the table 'Rest Periods' at the front of the book as a guide). Power is then increased by 10 per cent in the next round, followed by another rest. Continue to work through this training drill, adding on 10 per cent of power each time until you build up to 100 per cent of your maximum power.

You'll notice as you progress through the different ranges that your muscles will start to tire, so in reality you'll probably be striking the pads with less final power than had you started round one using 100 per cent. The idea behind this drill

Fig. 116   Punching with reduced power.

Fig. 117   Reduced power jab.

is that you develop the muscles and body movement used when striking through repetition of technique and increasing the workload each round; a similar principle to weight training (Figs 116–118).

Training Drill 5

Squat Kick

This training drill will develop explosive power in the legs, a key element required when kicking. Position yourself in front of a kick shield or punch bag and adopt a neutral stance (that is, both legs should be on the same line). Place your fingers on your temples and squat down so that your elbows and knees touch. Be careful not simply to lean forward at this stage, but instead keep the back straight and bend the legs.

From here, drive yourself back up to standing, at the same time kicking the kick shield or punch bag with a front kick using as much power as you can deliver. Instantly squat back down again and repeat the exercise, kicking off alternate legs each time (Figs 119 and 120).

Fig. 118   Reduced power cross.

Fig. 119   The squat.

Fig. 120   The front kick.

Training Drill 6

Sprawl Kick

This training drill works along similar lines to the last one, but is a lot tougher. From a left lead (Fig. 121), drop into a wrestler's sprawl (Fig. 122), immediately spring back up (Fig. 123) and kick the shield with a round kick (Fig. 124). I would suggest you work this one using one leg at a time before moving on to the other leg. So, for example, you might do 1min only kicking with your left (lead) leg, then repeat the drill using the right (rear leg) for round two.

Training Drill 7

Squat Jumping Kick (Straight)

Face your partner in a left lead fighting stance. Squat down, keeping your left leg in front and explode up into the air striking the pad with a jumping front kick. Switch the legs with each kick.

For this drill you can either work with a training partner holding a focus pad or similar small

Fig. 121   Start position.

Fig. 122   Drop into a
wrestler's sprawl.

Fig. 123   Spring back up.

Fig. 124   Round kick to
the kick shield.

Fig. 125   Squat down.

Fig. 126   Spring into the air and front kick.

target, or you can work alone with a hanging maize ball. Both will give you the same effect (Figs 125 and 126).

Training Drill 8

Squat Jumping Kick (Circular)
This training drill is simply a variation of the last one. Instead of kicking straight up as you jump, you now kick in a circular motion using a kick such as a round kick.

Observe how the pads are now held in order to absorb the impact of the kick better. This training drill also works well using a punch bag if a training partner is not available (Figs 127 and 128).

Training Drill 9

Isolated Techniques
This simple training drill involves isolating kicking techniques and training them with full power on a large target such as a kick shield or a punch bag. Your objective with this drill is to train each kick on its own for a period of time, or for a number of repetitions (I would suggest you keep this figure high, regardless of your level) and slow down the speed of each attack so you can be sure to work each kick properly.

As a guide for this drill, you need to be striking the target with your chosen kick, then taking a second to reset yourself before striking again. Don't get caught in the common trap of trying to do as many kicks as you can, as this style of training develops speed over power. Figs 129 to 131 show examples of the kind of kicks you should be using for this drill.

Training Drill 10

Seated Kicking
This next training drill is going to work your explosive power, but it will also have a secondary effect on your cardio fitness. For that reason, I would advise that you slow the pace of each kick so that you don't burn out before your muscles do.

Fig. 127   Squat down.

Fig. 128   Spring into the air and round-kick.

Fig. 129   Isolate the front kick with power.

Fig. 130   Isolate the round kick with power.

You can work this drill one of two ways. Either start from a seated position (Fig. 134) and by supporting yourself with your right side, drive a round kick into the target as hard as you can (Fig. 135), before returning to the seated position once more. Or, for a more advanced total body workout, start in a push-up position (Fig. 132), perform a push-up (Fig. 133), jump into a seated position by driving your right leg through to the front (this takes some skill in itself), then kick the target before jumping back into a push-up position and repeating once more.

Training Drill 11

Seated Punches

This drill will help you to develop power in the legs. It works by holding yourself in a seated position while performing punching techniques out in front. The traditional martial artist will know this particular seated position as a horse-riding stance (Karate) or a sitting stance (Tae Kwon Do), but we'll simply refer to it as a squat. In

Fig. 131   Isolate the side kick with power.

Fig. 132   From a push-up position.

Fig. 133   Perform a push-up.

Fig. 134   Jump through to a seated position.

Fig. 135   Perform a seated round kick.

Fig. 136   Perform a left-hand hip punch from a squat position.

Fig. 137   Perform a right-hand hip punch.

order to perform this correctly, you need to place your heels flat on the floor, your thighs parallel to the floor (so that if you placed a broom handle on the legs it wouldn't roll off) and keep your back straight (do not lean forward).

From this position, place your left hand out in front and your right hand on your hip and by simulating a hip punch, perform as many strikes as you can for your level (refer to the table 'Training Times/Repetitions' at the front of the book as a guide). Figs 136 and 137 demonstrate this for you.

Training Drill 12

High, Middle, Low

Although predominantly working the legs, this drill will help develop balance, as well as providing an upper body workout due to the addition of the punches.

Fig. 138   Perform a standing jab.

Fig. 139   Drop a level and cross punch.

Fig. 140   Drop a level and jab.

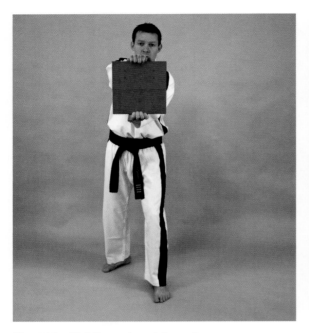

Fig. 141   Holding a break board.

Fig. 142   Ready position for the kick.

Fig. 143   Side-kick through a break board.

From your upright position, send out a jab, or any other lead-hand technique of your choice (Fig. 138). From here, immediately drop a level (to waist height) and send out a cross punch or any other rear-hand technique. Be sure to work the full range of motion as you punch (Fig. 139). Drop a final level to bring you to around knee height and send out another lead-hand technique (Fig. 140).

You can then come straight back to the start position or, for a tougher workout, work back up to standing one level at a time. Repeat this drill for a set amount of time based on your level of fitness (refer to the table 'Training Times/ Repetitions' at the front of the book as a guide).

Training Drill 13

Board-Breaking

Although this training drill is a great developer of power, the break board also helps to develop focus and targeting, which we'll look at in Chapter 7, 'Developing Targeting'. There are several types and strengths of break board, so if you are going to incorporate a break board into your training repertoire, be sure to choose a good one and remember that 'expensive' does not necessarily mean 'good'.

The strength of the break board is usually signified by its colour. A rough guide by which to judge a board's strength is the lighter the colour, the lower the resistance. So you could expect a white board to be easier to break than a black board, for example. Just ensure you check carefully when buying.

I would also recommend a holder to support the board as you strike it. However, these can be quite expensive. A cheaper option is to get a training partner (or two) to hold the board for you. Just ensure they don't move or recoil their arms back as you strike, as the board won't break if this happens. Fig. 141 shows how to hold a break board. Figs 142 and 143 show a kick in action.

Training Drill 14

Weighted Gloves

Weight training is a great way to develop power in your techniques. Training with some kind of weight causes the muscles to work harder, which in turn helps to develop them further. If you are going to use weighted gloves in your training, strict guidelines must be adhered to:

- use gloves that allow you to adjust the level of weight. Most weighted gloves have sandbags that can be added and removed. Avoid ones with a fixed weight that could be too heavy or too light in the beginning
- *never* punch at full speed while wearing weighted gloves; this is a surefire way to cause injury
- *never* punch a target wearing weighted gloves; only punch the air and at a reduced speed (*see* point above).

My suggestion for weighted gloves is to use them as part of a shadow sparring session, punching at a reduced speed and power for a set time period only (see the Training Times/Repetitions table at the front of the book).

Fig. 144   The lead hook with weighted glove.

Fig. 145   The cross with weighted glove.

Fig. 146   The jab with resistance band.

Fig. 147   The cross with resistance band.

You can also wear weighted gloves when running as the additional weight they offer during this type of training will help to develop your cardiovascular training even further.

If you don't have access to weighted gloves then you can substitute them for light hand weights or a similar, easy to hold weighted object (Figs 144 and 145)

Training Drill 15

Resistance Band

A resistance band offers a slightly different level of development to the previous training drill by adding resistance to the techniques. To use a resistance band when developing punches, simply wrap the band around your hands and take it around your back as shown. Each time you punch, the resistance that the band adds to each technique will force the muscles to work harder.

As the resistance band does not add any extra weight, the arms won't tire in the same way as they would for the previous training drill, so now the exact muscles that you use when performing each technique get worked fully (Figs 146 and 147).

You can also use the resistance band in a similar way to help develop your kicks (Fig. 148).

Fig. 148   The round kick with resistance band and training partner.

Training Drill 16

Kneeling Punches

A great deal of the power in a punch, if thrown properly, comes from the legs and hips. Therefore, if we take these out of the equation we are only left with upper body power. Naturally, if you develop the upper body power in a punch, the punch will become more powerful when the legs and hips are added back in again.

To help develop power in the upper body, we're going to reduce the work of the lower body for this drill. You can either train this drill by isolating a certain technique, or by working random hand techniques for a set time, based on your level of fitness (Fig. 149).

Take this drill a step further by removing the work of the lower body altogether and sit on the floor in front of your target (this can be either a training partner or a punch bag that reaches to the floor). Train it in the same way as the last drill (Fig. 150).

Fig. 149   Punches from kneeling position.

Training Drill 17

Slow Kicking

Performing a technique slowly is a great way to develop the muscles used during that technique. A kick is a great technique to use for this drill, as the weight of a leg is around 9–10 per cent of the weight of the entire body, so without adding any other resistance to it, simply lifting your own leg up and down slowly will help to develop the leg muscles for the full range of motion.

To assist with balance, support yourself with something sturdy such as a chair (as shown). Take the leg from a guard position (Fig. 151), to a chambered position (Fig. 152), to full extension (Fig. 153) and hold for 1sec, before bringing the leg back down again. Ideally, try to remove the chair from the drill as quickly as possible, so that you do not become too dependent on it. Each rep should take about 10sec to perform; anything less means you are kicking too fast.

An advanced variation on this drill involves the use of ankle weights. Adopt the same rules as in training drill 14 when using ankle weights (Figs 154 to 156).

Fig. 150   Punches from seated position.

Fig. 151   Slow kicking start position.

Fig. 152   Chamber the leg.

Fig. 153   Extend the kick and hold.

Fig. 154   Start position with ankle weights.

Fig. 155   Chamber the leg.

Fig. 156   Extend the kick and hold.

5 Developing Speed

Speed is a key element when it comes to the attack. If your attacking speed is slow, there's a greater chance the opponent will see it coming. If your attacking speed is fast, however, there's more chance your techniques will land with little opportunity for the opponent to defend them. Certain techniques are better for speed, whereas others are designed more for power. The backfist strike, for example, is quite possibly the fastest hand technique in the kickboxer's arsenal and, if used correctly, has the ability to land before the opponent even sees it coming. The cross punch is a great complement to the backfist and, when used in combination, the end result can be quite devastating.

The general thought process of a skilled fighter is to use fast techniques to cover distance and probe through the opponent's defences, thereby opening up the opponent in order to send a more powerful finishing shot. The jab is probably the most frequently used hand technique due to its versatility. As it is nearer to the target, it initially has less distance to travel compared to, say, the cross punch, therefore it is naturally going to be faster as it has less distance to cover. Not only that, but because it is a straight attacking punch, it can also be used long range. A lot of the drills in this chapter will focus on the backfist strike and the jab to help enhance these two incredible attacking tools.

Developing speed is certainly an essential element. However, we also need to develop *explosive speed* and there's a difference. If a fighter threw fifty punches in 30sec (a neat feat in itself), that fighter would be considered to have incredible hand speed and rightly so. However, imagine if a fighter threw just one punch, but that punch was so fast the opponent did not see it coming, could not defend against it and got knocked out (some-thing that happens quite a lot in the fighting world). That fighter would be consider to have incredible *explosive* speed, that is, the ability to go from stationary to landing a punch, or barrage of punches. As fighters, we need both types of speed. However, not all fighters have this dual ability.

A great example of explosive speed at the very highest level can be seen at most point fighting competitions. Lyoto Machida, UFC (Ultimate Fighting Championship) Light Heavyweight Champion at the time of writing has his founda-tions in Karate, where the style of fighting is based on explosive, single shots. This approach to fighting has helped him to attain one of the most prestigious and sought-after titles in the world.

IMPORTANT − Ensure that you have warmed up and stretched correctly before moving on to the following training drills. Use the training guides at the start of the book to assist you.

Training Drill 1

Explosive Exercises

The idea behind this training drill is to take a specific exercise such as push-ups and do as many as you can in a set time (30sec, for exam-ple). Keep a record of your progress and try to beat your previous score on the next attempt. You can either work this drill on your own, or with a training partner (Figs 157 and 158), attempting to beat their score for each round. When you are no longer able to beat your previous score, increase the time period by 15sec.

I would suggest working a minimum of three types of exercise and a maximum of six at any one time. Choose from the exercises below:

Fig. 157   Working with a partner.

Fig. 158   Touch the chest to their fist.

- push-ups – upper body
- sit-ups – upper abdominals
- hyperextensions – lower back
- squats – legs
- burpees – full body
- star jumps – full body
- tuck jumps – legs
- jumping squats – legs
- leg raises (lying) – lower abdominals
- bouncing leg raises (standing) – legs

Training Drill 2

Explosive Punches

This drill works along similar lines to the previous one, but uses punches instead of exercises. You can either isolate a single punch (such as the jab), work double punch combinations (such as the jab, cross), or put together multiple combinations (Figs 159 and 160).

Fig. 159   Explosive punching – the jab.

Fig. 160   The cross.

Training Drill 3

Explosive Kicks

As above, but using kicks (Figs 161 and 162).

Training Drill 4

Ten and Change

For this drill, choose a technique or a combina- tion of techniques and perform ten of them as fast as you can. As soon as you have done ten, switch the pads and your partner repeats the drill. Work this drill for a specific time limit (60sec, for example), attempting to perform as many changeovers as possible. Aim to beat your overall score the next time you perform the drill. When you are no longer able to beat your score, increase the time limit by 30sec (Figs 163 and 164).

Fig. 161   Pad position for the explosive round kick.

Fig. 162   The explosive round kick.

Fig. 163   Ten and change – the cross.

Fig. 164   Ten and change – the hook.

Fig. 165   Beat your partner start position.

Fig. 166   Attempt to beat your partner.

Fig. 167   Hand slap start position.

Fig. 168   Slap the hand.

Fig. 169   Foot slap start position.

Fig. 170   Slap the foot.

Training Drill 5

Beat Your Partner 1

For this drill, you need to hit the pad with a chosen (single) technique before your partner can move the pad out of the way. The pad feeder must remain stationary until you commit to your attack and only then can they move. Add an element of competition by being the first person to score ten (for example, ten hits or ten misses). Introduce a forfeit for the person who loses (Figs 165 and 166).

Training Drill 6

Hand Slap

This time, your objective is to hit the pad with a

specific hand technique, then retract your hand before your partner can slap it. An alternative to the above competition is to perform ten attacks, keeping a note of the total number of successful attacks, then switch the pads around so that your partner tries to beat your score. The loser does a forfeit (Figs 167 and 168).

Training Drill 7

Foot Slap

As above, but using kicks this time (Figs 169 and 170).

Training Drill 8

Move Back

This drill involves kicking a kick shield before your partner can move out of the way of the attack. The pad feeder must remain stationary until they see you move. This drill will not only develop your attacking speed, but will also help to remove the telegraph (*see* information box) associated with kicking, as it is probably the telegraph that the pad feeder will see first (Figs 171 and 172).

Training Drill 9

Beat Your Partner 2

A group of three is needed here – one pad feeder and two punchers. The pad feeder stands in-between the two punchers holding the pads out as shown (change the angle of the pads to match the techniques being used). On the pad feeder's command, both punchers attempt to hit the pad as fast as possible. The pad feeder awards a point to the person with the fastest attack and starts again (Figs 173 and 174). Work this drill for a total of ten attacks, then switch the pads around. The person with the lowest score at the end of the round does a forfeit.

Fig. 171   Move-back drill start position.

Fig. 172   Move back when you see the kick.

Spotting the Telegraph

When a fighter telegraphs a technique, they generally make some additional pre-strike movement that an experienced fighter will be able to pick up on and use to their advantage. (It is so named because you might as well 'write your opponent a telegraph telling them what you're about to do'.) Telegraphing a kick, for example, might involve a simple step up with the back foot, or a slight drop of the guard prior to kicking. Typical telegraphs for a punch usually involve pulling back the attacking arm, or a roll of the shoulder on the punching side.

There are many more tell-tale signs that give away the fact that your opponent is about to attack if you look for them. Your job as a fighter is to spot them as they happen, determine from that particular movement which attack is most likely to follow and be ready for it as it happens, that is, being proactive instead of reactive.

For example, a step up probably means a kick is on its way. If the opponent is front on as they step, it is more likely to be a front-on attack such as a front kick. However, if they start to swing their leg as they step, then it's possibly an axe kick that's coming. This simple but effective principle will be the difference between you getting hit by an attack, or knowing what's coming and defending against it.

Fig. 173 Start position for beat your partner 2.

Fig. 174 Strike the pad faster than your partner.

Training Drill 10

Beat Your Partner 3

As above, but now the punchers face the pads. You can opt to increase the distance between the punchers and the pad feeder, so that the punchers have to sprint to the pads before they can hit them (Figs 175 and 176).

Training Drill 11

Turn Around

This time, the puncher faces away from the pad feeder in a fighting stance. When the pad feeder taps the puncher on the back, they turn as fast as possible and attack the pads. Either use a set attack, or opt to attack the pads based on how they are held for that round (Figs 177 to 179).

Fig. 175   Start position for beat your partner 3.

Fig. 176   Strike the pad faster than your partner.

Fig. 177   Start position for the turn around drill.

Fig. 178   Tag your partner with the pad.

Fig. 179   Turn and strike the pad.

Training Drill 12

Belt Tag

A fun game that not only helps to develop explosive speed, but also helps to develop footwork, movement and defences, as well as introducing you to sparring. The objective of this drill is to tag your partner's belt (or mid-line) as often as possible in a set time while attempting to stop your partner tagging your belt. Once you become familiar with this, you can introduce shoulder tag and knee tag to vary the attacking levels. A point system can be introduced to make the drill more interesting. The first to score ten points is the winner:

- shoulder = one point
- belt = two points
- knee = three points.

Again, introduce forfeits for the losing fighter (Figs 180 and 181).

Fig. 180   Belt tag.

Fig. 181   Tag the belt.

Training Drill 11

Broken Rhythm

The pad feeder starts with the pads on their chest (Fig. 182). As they present a pad, the puncher attempts to hit the pad as fast as they can with the correct technique, based on how the pad is held (Fig. 183). The pad feeder then places the pad back on their chest and using broken rhythm (that is, randomly) presents the next one. This drill can also be used with kicks.

Training Drill 12

Pad Throw

The pad feeder throws the pad into the air and the puncher attempts to do as many punches as possible before the pad hits the floor. Isolated punches or combinations can be used and you can either set the attack each round (for example, only use the jab and the cross), or allow the

Fig. 182   Place the pads on the chest.

Fig. 183   Present the pad using broken rhythm.

Fig. 184 Throw the pad in the air.

Fig. 185 Start punching as the pad falls.

Fig. 186 Perform as many punches as possible before the pad hits the floor.

puncher to use free play (any technique or combination of techniques that they want). The person that manages to do the most punches wins the round. You can also use kicks to perform this training drill (Figs 184 to 186).

Training Drill 13

Call It

For this drill, you number specific techniques and each time that number is called you perform the corresponding technique as fast as possible. This drill not only develops your physical speed, but also helps to develop your processing speed (the ability to react to a command), as you have to translate the number into the correct technique before you can hit the pads. Start off with one number and once you become familiar with this, the caller can start adding numbers together. Use the chart to help you number the techniques.

Training Drill 14

Reaction Time

This time, the pad feeder starts with the pads at their chest (Fig. 187). They then call a technique as they move the pad into place. The puncher needs to react as fast as possible, striking the pad with the correct technique (Fig. 188). The pad feeder can add an element of competition by only holding the pad in place for a few seconds (vary the time based on the level of the puncher) before bringing it back to the chest again.

The same drill can be used to develop kicking speed by isolating the legs only, or you can work both hands and legs at the same time so as to push your partner even further.

Suggested Numbers for Call It

Number	Technique
1	backfist strike
2	jab
3	cross
4	lead hook
5	rear uppercut
6	lead front kick
7	lead round kick
8	lead side kick
9	spinning back kick
10	spinning hook kick

Training Drill 15

One for One Kicks

This final drill adds an element of competition between you and your training partner, both as the kicker and as the pad feeder. You both hold a focus pad on the left hand. The first person kicks the pad as fast as they can, then immediately holds their pad out to receive a kick. The second person kicks that pad as fast as possible and repeats the drill. Continue for a set time (refer to the table 'Training Times/Repetitions' at the front of the book as a guide), aiming to hit the other pad as fast as possible and outpace your partner. You can also vary the heights, pad positions and kicks (Figs 189 and 190).

Fig. 187   Hold the pads to the chest.

Fig. 188   Strike the pad as it's presented.

Fig. 189   Kick your partner's pad.

Fig. 190   Your partner returns the kick.

6 Developing Timing

Timing and speed generally go hand in hand. You could be the fastest puncher in the world, but if your timing is poor, then all those lightning-fast punches may simply miss or bounce harmlessly off the guard of your opponent. It could also be argued that as long as your timing is good, speed is irrelevant, as a successfully timed attack is going to land, regardless of how fast it is thrown. As fighters, we have a huge advantage if we have both elements in place, so even if you choose to study nothing else in this book, make sure you study speed and timing.

So what *is* timing? Timing is the ability to send a technique (or barrage of techniques) at exactly the right moment in a fight, so that the chances of the attack landing are greatly increased. The advantage here is obvious and timing works not only in attack, but equally as well in defence. Mistime your defence and the attack is going to land.

Timing is an element used a lot when counter-fighting, as the counter-fighter will wait for their opponent to attack before blocking or evading, then returning with an attack of their own. A well-timed counter-attack will more than likely

Fig. 191   Both fighters face each other.

Fig. 192   Fighter A sprawls while Fighter B kicks.

land, whereas a poorly timed counter-attack usually results in the two fighters clashing and the fight becoming 'scrappy' (a term used a lot in the fighting world when the skill and technique in a fight goes out the window and both fighters temporarily enter survival mode).

This chapter will help you to develop incredible timing, which, when combined with explosive speed, will ensure your attacks are unstoppable.

IMPORTANT – Ensure that you have warmed up and stretched correctly before moving on to the following training drills. Use the training guides at the start of the book to assist you.

Training Drill 1

Front Kick, Sprawl

Both fighters face each other in a fighting stance (Fig. 191). On the command 'three, two, one, go', Fighter A starts sprawling, while fighter B performs alternate leg front kicks over the head of fighter A (Fig. 192). Continuous sprawling is quite tough, so perform this drill for a set time based on the fitness levels of both fighters (refer to the table 'Training Times/Repetitions' at the front of the book as a guide).

Just be aware that this drill requires great timing from both parties, as a poorly timed kick or sprawl will most likely result in a front kick in the face.

Training Drill 2

Leg Jump

This drill not only takes great timing, but also requires a great deal of trust between both parties. Starting in position 1 (Fig. 193), fighter A jumps into the air as high as possible, while fighter B opens their legs (Fig. 194) just wide enough for fighter A to land back inside (Fig. 195). As soon as fighter A touches down, they spring back up again as high as possible, as fighter B closes their legs (Fig. 196), enabling fighter A to land back into position 1 again (Fig. 197). Continue jumping and opening/closing the legs for a set time based on fitness levels (refer to the table 'Training Times/Repetitions' at the front of the book as a guide).

Fig. 193   Fighter A stands over Fighter B's legs.

Fig. 194   Fighter A jumps as Fighter B opens their legs.

Fig. 195 Fighter A lands inside the legs of Fighter B.

Fig. 196 Fighter A jumps and Fighter B closes their legs.

Fig. 197 Fighter A lands back into the start position.

Training Drill 3

Broken Rhythm

To start this drill, the pad feeder holds the pads against their chest (Fig. 198). Without any verbal instruction, the pad feeder randomly holds a pad out while keeping the other one on the chest. The puncher hits the pad with the most appropriate technique as soon as it is presented (Fig. 199). The pad feeder then retracts the pad, placing it back on the chest and presents the other pad at the same time for the puncher to hit (Fig. 200).

This same drill can be used to work legs only, or to combine hands and legs together. Work the drill for a set time based on fitness levels (refer to the table 'Training Times/ Repetitions' at the front of the book as a guide).

Fig. 198   Face your partner.

Fig. 199   Uppercut the focus pad.

Training Drill 4

Three-Beat Rhythm

Both fighters hold a focus pad on their right hand. Fighter A strikes the pad with a jab (beat 1) and without pausing fighter B immediately returns the jab to the pad of fighter A (beat 2), with fighter A striking back once more (beat 3) straight after that. Switch the roles so that fighter B attacks first (beat 1), then fighter A returns the attack (beat 2), and fighter B finishes the attack (beat 3). Continue the attacks for a set time based on fitness levels (refer to the table 'Training Times/Repetitions' at the front of the book as a guide). Figs 201 to 203 show the first stage of this drill.

Once you become familiar with this drill you can change the techniques and even add in defences. The key is to work three techniques between two fighters as fast as possible.

The table 'Three-Beat Rhythm Combinations' shows some combinations that could be used with this drill. Add any others that you feel are appropriate.

Fig. 200   Hook the focus pad.

Three-Beat Rhythm Combinations

Technique No. 1	Technique No. 2	Technique No. 3
jab	jab	jab
jab	cross	jab
jab	defend (any attack)	jab
front kick	front kick	front kick
front kick	round kick	front kick
front kick	jab	front kick
defend (a jab)	defend (a jab)	defend (a jab)

As you can see, there are many possible combinations, so don't get too caught up in these. The objective of this drill is to develop your timing by working a fast and explosive three-beat rhythm with your partner.

Training Drill 5

Double Kicks

Double-kicking drills are great for developing timing, because in a fight you need to time your attacks so that the second kick lands as a result of your opponent reacting to your initial attack. When working this drill, ensure that there is a definite change between the first and second attacks. You will also find the drill works far better if you are able to keep the leg in the air between attacks. Figs 204 to 206 show a double round kick in attack, kicking to the body initially in order to create a reaction from the opponent (in this case, dropping the guard to defend the kick to the body), before timing a second attack to the head once the guard has been lowered.

The table 'Double-Kick Combinations' shows some excellent double-kick combinations that work well together.

Fig. 201   Fighter A performs a jab.

Fig. 202   Fighter B returns the jab.

Fig. 203   Fighter A attacks again.

Double-Kick Combinations

Kick 1	Kick 2
round kick to the body	round kick to the head
hook kick to the head	round kick to the head (opposite side)
round kick to the head	hook kick to the head (opposite side)
front kick to the body	round kick to the head
axe kick to the head	side kick to the body
side kick to the body	axe kick to the head
axe kick to the head	round kick to the head (opposite side)

Fig. 204   Strike the first pad.   Fig. 205   Keep the knee high.   Fig. 206   Strike the second pad.

Training Drill 6

One for One Techniques Version 1

This drill involves attacking the body of your partner with an isolated technique, then receiving one back. The objective is to keep the pace fast and controlled so that there's little to no pause between techniques. Also try to vary the technique each time (Figs 207 to 209).

As gloves are not worn during this drill, avoid strikes to the face. An alternative version involves the use of boxing gloves and head guards, thereby allowing head shots to be incorporated. I would suggest you train this drill in three different ways:

- hands only
- legs only
- hands and legs together.

Fig. 207   Attack the open area of your partner.

Fig. 208   Your partner returns the attack.

Fig. 209   You attack again.

Training Drill 7

One for One Techniques Version 2

This drill is the same as the previous one, except that you now strike focus pads instead of your partner. This drill is slightly more advanced, in that the striking technique is now governed by your training partner and the way they hold their pad for you to hit (Figs 210 to 212).

Training Drill 8

Triangle Kicking

Ideally in a group of three, one person holds a kicking shield and the other two stand either side. One person starts by kicking the shield with a round kick and as soon as they retract their leg the other person kicks with the same technique. The objective is to time your kick so that, without pausing in-between, you are able to bounce your kicking leg off the floor and then strike the kick shield without clashing legs with your partner (Figs 213 and 214).

Fig. 210   Attack your partner's pad.

Fig. 211   Your partner attacks back.

Fig. 212   You attack again.

Fig. 213   Kick the kick shield.

Fig. 214   Your training partner kicks the kick shield.

You can add an element of competition and also cardio training into this drill by trying to outpace your partner. Work this drill for a set time based on ability levels (refer to the table 'Training Times/Repetitions' at the front of the book as a guide), then switch places with the person to your left.

Training Drill 9

Hand Slap

Face your partner in a fighting stance. The objective with this drill is to touch your partner on the chest before they can slap your hand. This drill will actually train two elements: speed, as the attacking person needs to use explosive speed to tag the chest without getting their hand slapped; and timing, as the defending person needs to use timing in order to slap the hand of the attacker at some point before it is returned back to the guard (Fig. 215).

Fig. 215   Attempt to slap the attacking hand.

Fig. 216   Foot slap start position.

Fig. 217   Attempt to slap the attacking foot.

70

Training Drill 10

Foot Slap

This drill is similar to the previous one, but this time the objective is to kick out at your partner, while retracting the kick before they can grab or slap your foot (depending on the rules that have been set). My suggestion is to aim to kick at your partner, but not actually to kick them. Sometimes when working speed drills you naturally find that power is also present, so an accidentally timed kick to the body may come a little harder than originally planned (Figs 216 and 217).

Training Drill 11

Sport Kickboxing Drills

The attacking techniques in a sport kickboxing competition need to be incredibly explosive and precisely timed, so this training drill provides an ideal opportunity to work three of the most appropriate attacks.

Fig. 218   Distance yourself from the target.

Fig. 219   Explode in with the first attack.

Fig. 220   Land the second attack.

Fig. 221   Strike the pad with a jab.

Backfist/Reverse Punch Combo   The pad feeder holds the focus pads as shown in Fig. 218. From a distance, explode in with a backfist strike to the head pad (Fig. 219) and as soon as the backfist connects, send a long-range reverse punch to the body pad (Fig. 220).

Jab/Ridgehand Strike Combo   The pad feeder holds the focus pads as shown. Send a jab to the head pad (Fig. 221), and, without pausing, immediately send a reverse ridgehand strike to the other pad (Fig. 222).

Backfist/Reverse Punch/Ridgehand Strike Combo   The pad feeder holds the pads as shown in Fig. 223. Send a long-range backfist strike to the head pad with full commitment (Fig. 224). Immediately send a reverse punch to the body pad (Fig. 225) and, without pausing, send a reverse ridgehand strike to the head pad (Figs 226 and 227).

Fig. 222   Follow with a ridgehand strike.

Fig. 223   Distance yourself from the pad.

The key thing with these attacks is that they require timing in order to land. The initial attack is designed to create a reaction in your opponent in much the same way as the double kicks do (training drill 5). As soon as your opponent reacts to your initial attack the second (or third) attack finds its mark. If your timing is slightly out here though, your opponent will have recovered enough to defend against your next attack.

Fig. 224   Send the backfist strike.

Fig. 225   Send the reverse punch.

Fig. 226   Prime the ridgehand strike.

Fig. 227   Send the ridgehand strike.

Fig. 228   Parry the attack.

Fig. 229   Send back a jab.

Fig. 230   Parry the jab.

Training Drill 12

Parry, Attack Version 1

Face your partner in a left-lead fighting stance. As your partner throws a jab toward your face, parry it with your rear hand, knocking it off the centreline (Fig. 228). Immediately send back a jab (Fig. 229). Your partner returns the parry (Fig. 230). Continue to flow the drill back and forth for a set time.

Training Drill 13

Parry, Attack Version 2

This time, send a cross punch while your partner parries the attack with their lead hand (Fig. 231). They then return the attack, which you parry (Fig. 232). Flow the drill as in drill 12.

Fig. 231   Parry the cross.

Fig. 232   Your partner returns the cross, which you parry.

Training Drill 14

Parry, Attack Version 3

In version 3, your partner throws a jab, which you parry with your lead hand (Fig. 233), then attack back with any technique (Fig. 234). Your partner then attacks with any technique, which you parry (Fig. 235). You attack back again with any technique, or combination of techniques (Figs 236 and 237). Flow the drill as before.

Fig. 233   Parry the attack.

Fig. 234   Counter with any hand.

Fig. 235   Parry the attack.

Fig. 236   Counter the attack.

Fig. 237   Finish with a second counter.

Training Drill 15

Counter-Kick

Your partner stands facing you armed with a
kicking shield (Fig. 238). They then rush you,
simulating a 'blitzing' style attack. As you see
them move, time your attack to send a stopping
kick, such as a side kick, into the pad (Fig. 239).
Kicks that also work well as stopping techniques
are the back kick, as shown in figs 240 and 241,
and the front kick (not shown).

Fig. 238   Face the kick shield.

Fig. 239 Stop the attack with a side kick.

Fig. 240 Face the kick shield.

Fig. 241 Stop the attack with a back kick.

Training Drill 16

Cross Punch

The same timing as used in drill 15 can be worked, using a cross punch in place of a kick.

The cross punch is an incredibly powerful attacking technique and due to the straight line of travel is an ideal weapon to use to stop a 'blitzing' style attack (Figs 242 and 243).

Fig. 242 Face the kick shield.

Fig. 243 Stop the attack using a cross punch.

7 Developing Targeting

The next element we're going to look at is targeting. From experience, the time when targeting becomes paramount is during sparring or fighting (competitive or street) and an inability to target your attacks successfully at this stage will more than likely result in you losing the fight. Time and time again I watch martial-arts students of all styles randomly throwing out kicks and punches because they believe that's what they should be doing. This attitude toward a fight will only serve to tire you out, wear you down and waste attacks. Not only that, but you also allow your opponent too many opportunities to defend and counter.

Tell-tale signs of a student not understanding targeting is randomly kicking and punching the air instead of their opponent. Admittedly, if your opponent is incredibly skilled they could easily evade all of your attacks, but in reality it is more likely that the student does not understand how to land an attack. The other sign, which I believe to be worse, is watching a student constantly attack the guard of their opponent. It is acceptable to attack the guard if you are planning to create a reaction from your opponent in order to then land a second or third technique, but when most of the follow-up attacks also land on the guard, you know the student is struggling to understand what they should be doing.

Successfully targeting an attack can finish a fight instantly. Alternatively, if it goes the distance and most of your attacks have landed on the scoring zones, you could win on points. Targeting your attacks also means you conserve energy, which is a good thing, particularly if your opponent burns out in the early stages of the fight. The final thing you'll find when you target your attacks is that it gives the opponent less of an opportunity to defend and counter. If you're planning to counter the next punch and that punch hits you square in the face with a combination of speed, timing and targeting, it takes a second to get your bearings back, which makes it a lot harder to target your counter-shot successfully. What it does do, is buy your opponent another second to land a few more shots, one of which could be the knockout.

IMPORTANT – Ensure that you have warmed up and stretched correctly before moving on to the following training drills. Use the training guides at the start of the book to assist you.

Training Drill 1

Ping-Pong Training

This drill is an inexpensive yet amazingly effective training aid to assist in developing your targeting skills. Simply attach a piece of string with sticky tape to a ping-pong ball and hang it from the ceiling at a height you're comfortable with. Then move around as if you were sparring, aiming to touch the ball each time you attack (Figs 244 to 246).

Suggested training methods for this are:

- isolate a technique
- isolate hands only
- isolate legs only
- work hands and legs together
- accumulating punches
- accumulating kicks – without putting the leg down.

Fig. 244   Face the ping-pong ball.

Fig. 245   Jab the target.

Fig. 246   Kick the target.

Training Drill 2

Spot Training 1

This drill involves hitting the centre spot of a focus pad with the correct striking part of the hand or foot. The pad feeder holds the pad out in front of you (Fig. 247). With your chosen kick or punch, strike the pad, aiming to hold the technique for 1sec in order to see how close you got to the centre spot (Fig. 248). Repeat this drill ten times before changing to another technique.

Fig. 247   Face the target.

Fig. 248   Strike the target on the focus pad.

Fig. 249   Kick the target on the kick shield.

Fig. 250   Strike the open area on the body.

Training Drill 3

Spot Training 2

This drill works along similar lines to the previous one. However, you may find it easier, when targeting your kicks, to strike a kick shield instead of a focus pad in the early stages. Once you can hit the centreline of a kick shield every time, reduce the size of the target (Fig. 249).

Training Drill 4

Double Kicks

The double technique is a great technique for developing your targeting. Instruct your partner to hold a stationary fighting stance. You then select a double-kick combination (use the table 'Double-Kick Combinations' in training drill 5, Chapter 6, 'Developing Timing', to assist with this). Then, with control, strike the target areas on your partner, while kicking around their guard (Figs 250 and 251).

Fig. 251   Strike the open area on the head.

Fig. 252   Strike the pad as it is in the air.

Fig. 253   The pad flies off.

To add variation to this drill, instruct your partner to change their guard randomly so that you are not always kicking the exact same spot with the same combinations.

Training Drill 5

Pad Throw

This drill can be quite a fun one, particularly when you add in the spinning and/or jumping spinning kicks. Just ensure you have plenty of room to practise this drill with nothing breakable in the near vicinity. Simply throw a focus pad into the air and attempt to strike it with your chosen technique before it hits the ground (Figs 252 and 253).

Training Drill 6

Slow Pads

This time, your pad feeder slowly moves the focus pads around using a continuous movement but keeping the pads held at the same angle. You then attempt to strike the pads as they are moving (Figs 254 to 256).

Fig. 254   Hit the pad as it is moved slowly.

Fig. 255   The jab hits the pad.

Fig. 256   The cross hits the pad.

Fig. 257   Toss a ball toward your partner.

Fig. 258   Strike the ball as it comes toward you.

An alternate version is to change the angle of the pads as they move so that you constantly have to change the attack due to the attacking angle. Work hands, legs, and hands and legs separately.

Training Drill 7

Ball Throw 1

For this drill, you will need a lightweight ball of any size (the smaller the ball, the harder the drill). Your partner throws the ball toward you (Fig. 257) and you then attempt to strike the ball with a chosen technique (Fig. 258). The skill here is striking the ball so that your partner can catch it again.

Training Drill 8

Ball Throw 2

A variation to the previous drill, which also adds in an element of competition by calling out the technique just before you throw the ball. This means that not only does your partner have to contend with striking the ball, but they can only do it using the technique you nominate. Do this ten times each and the person who is least consistent attracts a forfeit.

Training Drill 9

Pad Strike

This drill ideally requires two pad feeders, with the puncher stood in the middle (Fig. 259). Pad feeder 1 (in front) holds the pad at a different angle to pad feeder 2 (behind) and the puncher strikes the first pad with the appropriate technique (Fig. 260). They then turn and strike the other pad with the technique appropriate to the angle of this pad (Figs 261 and 262). After each attack, the pad feeders change the pad position.

Fig. 259   Stand between two pad feeders.

Fig. 260   Strike the first pad.

Fig. 261   Turn to face the other pad.

Fig. 262   Strike the second pad.

Work this drill for a set time based on your fitness levels (refer to the table 'Training Times/ Repetitions' at the front of the book as a guide).

Training Drill 10

Pad Strike 2

This works in the same way as the previous drill, except that now you hold two pads out and the puncher strikes both pads before turning to attack the rear ones (Figs 263 to 268).

Fig. 263 Stand between two pad feeders.

Fig. 264 Jab the first pad.

Fig. 265 Cross to the second pad.

Fig. 266 Turn to face the other pad feeder.

Fig. 267   Strike the first pad.

Fig. 268   Strike the second pad.

Training Drill 11

Spin Drill

This drill is another fun one, but with a serious side attached. Quickly spin your partner round ten times as shown in Figs 269 to 271, taking care that they don't fall over as a result of becoming light-headed. Your partner then needs to strike the pads with ten double punches, aiming to hit as accurately as possible with each punch (Figs 272 and 273). Make sure someone remains close by ready to catch them, just in case.

The effects of spinning your partner around in this manner is the closest you will get to the sensation of being dazed as a result of a punch on the chin/temple without actually having to get punched. If you can control the head spin and still target your shots, then you have a good chance of recovering from such an attack.

Fig. 269   Support your training partner.

Fig. 270   Spin them around.

Fig. 271   After the tenth spin, point them toward the pads.

Fig. 272   Strike the pads ten times using a jab ...

Fig. 273   ... and cross combination.

8 Developing Movement and Footwork

Movement and footwork are key elements in the martial-arts world, because they are what helps you to transition between attacks, avoid getting hit and close or create distance between you and your opponent. On top of this we also have balance, which is another essential element required of a fighter.

When we kick or punch, we need to be in total control of the full movement of that attack. Take a kick as a great example. I have witnessed many a fighter throw a kick in a fight, only to end up off-balance or in a different lead once the kick is complete. When you throw a kick, you need to be in total control from the point of execution, to the connection, to the recovery, to the landing. If you are not, you leave yourself vulnerable to a strong attack from your opponent, or limit your ability to attack or counter.

Time spent developing the foundations instead of rushing headlong into the fun stuff makes all the difference here. For this reason, this chapter is going to focus on developing the element that is only fully appreciated when watching the highest calibre of fighter do their thing.

IMPORTANT – Ensure that you have warmed up and stretched correctly before moving on to the following training drills. Use the training guides at the start of the book to assist you.

Training Drill 1

Accumulating Kicks

This first drill is a great one for developing balance. It can be done alone or with a training partner as your target. Alternatively, you can hit a punch bag or focus pads (which is also where your training partner comes in). Take one of the basic

Fig. 274   Send a round kick.

Fig. 275   Retract the kick.

Fig. 276   Kick again.

kicks (front kick, round kick, side kick or hook kick) and on the spot, perform one kick using your lead leg. Then repeat the exercise, but add an extra kick on the end before landing the leg. Continue up to ten kicks, then rest (Figs 274 to 276).

Training Drill 2

Circle attack

For this drill, you need a minimum of three pad feeders, with the puncher standing in the middle. Strike the first pad (Fig. 277) and then, using footwork and movement, turn so that you maintain your left lead and strike the second pad (Fig. 278). Turn again so that you strike the third pad (Fig. 279). Continue for a set period of time before changing positions.

You can isolate hands, legs, or hands and legs for this drill and the pad feeders can either maintain the same pad position, or vary it depending on the skill level of the person in the middle.

Fig. 277   Strike the first pad.

Fig. 278   Use footwork to attack the next pad.

Fig. 279   Use footwork to attack again.

Fig. 280   Face your partner.

Fig. 281   Follow your partner as they move.

Fig. 282   Turn as your partner turns.

Training Drill 3

Follow the Leader

This is a surprisingly simple footwork drill that will help you to develop agility in your movement. Face your partner as shown in Fig. 280. As your partner moves, one step at a time, you simply follow their movements (Figs 281 and 282). If they switch stance then you also switch stance to match them. It's basically a game of follow the leader using footwork only.

Training Drill 4

Legs Jump

This takes training drill 3 to the next level. The objective is to jump around your partner's legs without actually landing on them. Use footwork and quick changes to stay as light and agile as you can, as you transition between stances, leads and positions (Figs 283 to 287). Work this drill for a set time period based on your level of fitness (refer to the table 'Training Times/Repetitions' at the front of the book as a guide).

Fig. 283   Stand either side of your partner's legs.

Fig. 284   Jump in the air.

Fig. 285   Switch stance.

Fig. 286   Jump and turn.

Fig. 287   Change direction.

Training Drill 5

Simple Step

This drill involves the use of a simple step to cover the distance required for an attack to land. It's a great footwork move to use to help you cover distance when utilizing a straight punch to attack with. Stand at a distance from the pads (Fig. 288). Push off your rear leg and step forward with your lead leg (Fig. 289). Snap out a jab (Fig. 290), then a cross punch (Fig. 291). Follow your partner as they move around a little before repeating the drill.

Fig. 288   Stand at a distance from the pads.

Fig. 289   Push off your rear leg.

Fig. 290   Step forward and jab.

Fig. 291   Zone out and cross-punch.

Training Drill 6

Shuffle Step

This drill utilizes a shuffle step in order to cover distance so that a straight kick can land. Face the target as shown in Fig. 292. Shuffle-step by using a slight skipping motion to bring your rear foot up to the lead foot (Fig. 293), before driving the kick into the pads (Fig. 294). Be sure only to use a slight skip and not a jump with this one, otherwise it becomes more of a jumping step, which is not very efficient in terms of grace, speed and energy expenditure.

Training Drill 7

Slide Step

For this drill adopt a side-on stance as shown in Fig. 295. Slide the rear leg up to the front leg (Fig. 296) and strike the target with a side kick (Fig. 297). As with the shuffle step above, if you use a slight skipping motion with this one, you

Fig. 292   Face the kickshield.

Fig. 293   Shuffle-step up.

Fig. 294   Send the front kick.

Fig. 295   Stand at a distance to the target.

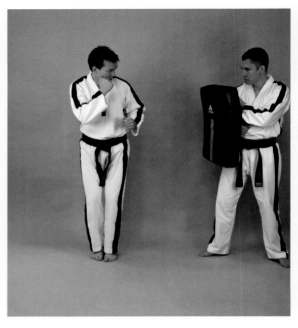

Fig. 296   Slide-step up.

Fig. 297   Side-kick the pad.

will find the step works exceptionally well for covering ground. It also works well in reverse when looking to make a quick retreat from an attack.

Training Drill 8

Cross Step

This footwork drill has the disadvantage of being a little slow, but the advantage of being extremely powerful. When using it for real, I would suggest you perform it to cover distance on a retreating opponent as you will soon catch them up. From a side-on stance again (Fig. 298), step behind your lead leg with your rear leg as shown in Fig. 299. From here, drive your kicking leg into the target, generating power from the hip (Fig. 300).

When performing the cross step, be sure to step behind the leg and not in front, to ensure there is no obstruction between the kicking leg and the supporting leg. Stepping in front is not only awkward, but a massive hindrance to the actual kick, as it removes the clear line of sight needed to make the kick effective.

Fig. 298   Stand at a distance to the target.

Fig. 299   Cross-step up.

Fig. 300   Side-kick the target.

Training Drill 9

Full Step

For this drill, we're going to change the angle so that you now adopt more of a front-on stance (Fig. 301). Step through with your rear leg (Fig. 302) and make a quick switch with the left hip, sending a round kick into the pads (Fig. 303). The key to this drill is to make the transition between the step and the kick as quick as possible. The full step, if done with speed, can be not only a very quick step, but moreover a very powerful one. Observe the rear foot position in Fig. 303. It's paramount to the success of this kick that you turn out the rear foot when kicking to ensure that the full energy of the lower body is behind the kick.

TOP LEFT: Fig. 301   Stand at a distance to the target.

BELOW LEFT: Fig. 302   Step through with the rear leg.

BELOW RIGHT: Fig. 303   Round-kick the pad.

TOP LEFT: Fig. 304   In a side-on stance.

TOP RIGHT: Fig. 305   Spin round.

BELOW RIGHT: Fig. 306   Round-kick the pad.

Training Drill 10

Spin Step

This time, stand side-on with the kick shield also side-on to your position (Fig. 304). From here, spin backward, bringing your rear leg to the front as shown in Fig. 305. Using the energy from the spin, continue bringing your body around and drive the kick into the pad using this momentum to generate additional power (Fig. 306). As before, observe the position of the supporting foot and ensure you turn into the kick to get the maximum amount of energy out of the kick.

Training Drill 11

Hop Step

Of all the footwork drills covered in this chapter, this one is probably the most efficient. It covers distance, generates power, utilizes speed and does away with the telegraph that lets most other footwork drills down. The telegraph is any pre-kick or punch movement a fighter does that might signal to their opponent what their next intention is. If done properly, the footwork drills contained in this chapter will be absent of any telegraph. However, where you might come unstuck is in the speed of their execution.

The hop step, however, is such a fast step that the first your opponent knows of it is when the kick has hit them. In order to perform the hop step correctly, work it as follows. In a fighting stance, draw your rear leg underneath your rear shoulder (Fig. 307). Bring the kicking leg off the floor as shown in Fig. 308 (this has been exaggerated to show how it works). Hop forward off your back leg toward your target (Fig. 309), landing the kick and the rear foot together (Fig. 310).

Admittedly, this will take some practice. However, with practice comes perfection and this footwork step is certainly worth persevering with.

Fig. 307   Stand at a distance to the target.

Fig. 308   Raise the kicking leg off the floor.

Fig. 309   Hop in close.

Fig. 310   Front kick the target.

Training Drill 12

Audio Pad Drill

This training drill will not only help you with your footwork and movement, but aid in developing your processing speed. Stand with your back toward your pad feeder as shown in Fig. 311. When your partner calls 'NOW', turn and strike the pads with the correct technique. Unlike previous drills when you maintain your left lead, this drill is all about speed. Therefore, the stance you end up in once you turn is the stance with which you strike the pads (Fig. 312). Simply use footwork to move into range of the pads and ensure correct body mechanics are used when striking.

Fig. 311   Turn your back on your partner.

Fig. 312   Turn to strike at the command.

Training Drill 13

Audio pad Drill 2

This drill works along similar lines to the previous one, except this time the pad feeder moves the pads around so as you turn now, you also need to determine the best striking tool for the position and angle of the pads.

Both drills work equally well with kicks. You could also work kicks and punches together.

Training Drill 14

Slow Kicking

Not only will this drill help to develop your balance, which is crucial to good movement and footwork, it will also strengthen the legs. When complemented with a good stretching routine, you will notice that this simple training drill greatly enhances the height, speed, power and balance of your kicking techniques.

Isolate a specific kick. I would suggest you focus on the front kick, round kick, side kick and hooking kick to start with. Once your balance

BELOW LEFT: Fig. 313   Start the slow-kicking drill.

TOP RIGHT: Fig. 314   Chamber the kick.

MIDDLE RIGHT: Fig. 315   Raise the knee high.

BOTTOM RIGHT: Fig. 316   Slowly extend the kick.

improves, add in the spinning hooking kick, but for now that might be too much of a challenge. Then using a count of 10sec as your guide, start from a fighting stance and slowly extend the kick out, aiming to be at full extension by the count of ten. Hold for 1sec, then retract the leg back to a fighting stance for another 10sec. Figs 313 to 316 show this in action.

To begin with you may have trouble with balance. If so, use a sturdy object such as the back of a chair to assist you until your balance improves. Try to get rid of the balance aid as quickly as possible though, as you may well become too reliant on it.

Training Drill 15

Machine-Gun Kicks 1

This is quite possibly one of the greatest drills to help you develop footwork, movement, balance and leg strength, as it combines all of the elements we are developing in this chapter. To begin with, instruct your training partner to stand still, ideally with their hands on their head. Next, slowly but methodically commence side-kicking around their body, using their mid-line as your guide (I would suggest pulling the kick slightly

short so as not actually to kick your partner). Each time you retract the kick, keep the leg chambered and move approximately 10 degrees anti-clockwise using a simple hop and kick again. Continue kicking all around the body of your partner until you reach your start point again. Rest for a second or two, then change legs and repeat the drill once more. Figs 317 to 319 show the drill in action.

The best kicks to use with this drill are side kicks, front kicks and round kicks.

Training Drill 16

Machine-Gun Kicks 2

This drill is a simple variation on drill 15 using the machine-gun kicking principle. Instead of kicking around the body of your training partner as you did with the last drill, this time travel in a straight line from one end of the room to the other, as if you were chasing a retreating opponent backward in a straight line. When you reach the opposite side, change legs and travel back to the start position.

To add an element of cardio to this drill, aim to travel back and forth a set number of times, for example three times there and back.

Fig. 317   Send your first kick.

Fig. 318   Use footwork to move around the body.

Fig. 319   Continue kicking as you move.

9 Developing the Defences

The next element we're going to develop is your ability to defend against an attack and although we've waited until Chapter 9 to look at it, it is actually an element that could come into play at any time. The ability to defend yourself is of major importance for so many obvious reasons. Rarely in a competitive fight or sparring match does a fighter solely attack. The only time I have ever witnessed it is when the initial attack finishes the fight, otherwise the fight generally takes on the role of both fighters attacking and attempting to defend.

Despite the importance of this element, most fighters fail to develop their defences properly and only actually train defensively when physically sparring (when you have little choice but to defend against an actual attack otherwise you get hit). I have seen many rookie fighters step into the world of sparring for their very first time and spend more time getting hit than hitting. It does not matter how good you are at hitting pads and combining all of the elements we've looked at so far, if you don't learn how to defend yourself *before* you start sparring, you're going to get hit.

The mentality of not developing your defences, then attempting to fight is similar to entering a competitive fight (or even just sparring) having never thrown a kick or a punch in your life. The reality is that even the best fighters in the world get hit. Ideally, what you are aiming to do when sparring or fighting is to minimize the damage you incur. This is where your skill at defending yourself comes into play. Any student not developing their defensive skill, because they don't realize they should be, because they get too caught up in seeing how hard they can hit at each training session (a common trait with the newbie student), or because their instructor isn't doing their job properly, is going to find the transition

from pad punching to sparring a very tough one indeed.

Spending all of your time focusing on your attacking skills and very little, if any, on your defensive skills is therefore a recipe for disaster, so this chapter will help you to develop this crucial element, bringing your defensive ability up to the level of your attacking ability. As an instructor, one of the things I do to check a student's ability level is to get them to shadow spar (shadow-sparring drills are covered in Chapter 12, 'Developing Shadowing'). Their main areas of development become evident when they only have imaginary opponents to fight against and, when shadowing, most students will revert back to what they know best. Anyone who has only ever practised attacking (pads, punch bags and so on) with little to no time spent practising their defences, will simply just spend their time attacking. How you train is how you fight …

IMPORTANT − Ensure that you have warmed up and stretched correctly before moving on to the following training drills. Use the training guides at the start of the book to assist you.

The following training drills can either be done using focus pads, coaching mitts or boxing gloves to attack with.

Training Drill 1

Cover 1

This training drill will help you to develop your ability to cover an attack. A cover is a simple fighting term for using your arms to cover the vulnerable area that is being attacked. As you will see from Fig. 320, the attacker is sending a straight attack (jab or cross) to the head. In response to this, the defender is using their arms to cover the head and absorb the attack. Although you are still getting hit, the arms can take a lot more 'punishment' than the face or body, so it's an ideal quick and simple defence when under pressure.

With bare knuckle or lightweight gloves such as MMA (mixed martial-art) ones, the hands are brought to the top of the head as shown. Boxing-style gloves restrict the opening of the hands, therefore the padded area is brought to the head instead. Just be sure not to place bare knuckles against the face or head when practising your covers without gloves on.

Train this drill by instructing your partner to throw slow, deliberate straight attacks at you with a steady rhythm. As you become confident with the defence, instruct your partner to throw attacks with broken rhythm. Work the drill for a time duration based on your ability level as shown in the table 'Training Times/Repetitions' at the start of the book.

Training Drill 2

Slipping

Slipping is a defence generally associated with a punch (for example, slipping a punch). In order to slip a punch, the punch needs to be travelling in a straight line (as opposed to a circular direction) and the head simply needs to move either left or right of the attack so that the punch sails past. The best way to envisage the correct movement required to slip a punch is to imagine the head and shoulders sitting on an A frame. Simply slide the shoulders down either side of the A to take the head off the centreline.

Fig. 321 shows how to slip a jab. The principle is the same for slipping a cross punch. Train this drill as advised for training drill 1. Once you become comfortable with it, add the cover technique intermittently.

Training Drill 3

Lean Back (Against a Punch)

This is an incredibly effective defence to use against a punch due to its simplicity and speed. Its versatility means that it will work just as well

Fig. 320   Defend a straight punch.

Fig. 321   Slip a straight punch.

Fig. 322   Lean-back defence.

Fig. 323   Lean back against a hook.

Fig. 324   Defend a circular attack.

Fig. 325   Alternate circular defence.

against a straight punch as it will against a circular or rising (uppercut) attack. As you will see from Fig. 322, the movement is very simple. In a fighting stance, simply lean back out of the way of the attack, keeping the lead shoulder high and the rear hand on the chin, just in case. Fig. 323 shows the defence in action against a hooking punch.

Train this drill as advised for training drill 1. Once you become comfortable with it, add the cover and the slip.

Training Drill 4

Cover 2

This alternate version of the cover is used to defend against a circular punch attack to the head and there are two variations of it. The first variation involves a single arm cover (Fig. 324), in which you keep the body and head facing forward and simply bring the arm on the same side of the attack, up to cover the punch or kick.

The second version involves turning the body into the attack and using both arms to defend with (Fig. 325). The position of the arms for the second version is the same as for the straight arm cover in training drill 1. Train this drill as above, adding the previous drills in when you become confident.

Training Drill 5

Cover 3

This cover is used to defend against a circular punching attack to the body (a hooking punch to the body, for example). Its effectiveness is down to the position of the natural guard and the speed at which you can move it into place. In order to cover this type of attack successfully, simply bring the elbow and hip together while keeping the fist on the chin or temple. You will need to crunch the body slightly as shown in Fig. 326 to help you achieve this position. This crunching movement actually helps in absorbing the energy of the attack.

Train this drill as advised in training drill 1 and when you are comfortable with it, add the other defences.

Fig. 326   Defence against a hooking punch to the body.

Training Drill 6

Cover 4

This cover is used to defend against a rising attack such as an uppercut or knee strike. In the same way as the cover used in training drill 1, when training/fighting bare knuckle, the open hands are placed on top of the head, as shown in Fig. 327. This prevents any risk of damage to the face or head as a result of the energy or power transfer through the actual guard due to bone-on-bone contact (that is, the bones of the knuckles contacting with the cheekbone or skull – depending where you hold the guard). If using boxing gloves to train with, the padded area of the glove can safely rest on the head or cheekbones because the protection that the gloves offer minimizes any risk of injury through bone-on-bone contact.

I would advise you to train this drill as described in training drill 1, adding the previous drills once comfortable.

Fig. 327   Defence against an uppercut.

Fig. 328   Roll under the hook.

Training Drill 7

Evasion

The evasion is a very effective defence against a circular attack when at close range. You normally find defences of this nature in boxing, when the fighters need to be close enough together for their punches to land, therefore constant head movement is important. In kickboxing or other stand-up arts that involve kicking, we have the luxury of distance brought about through the kicks, so we can move in close in order to punch, then move out of punching range in order to defend, yet still be in attacking range with the kicks.

As your training partner sends a hooking punch, roll in the same direction of the attack in order to avoid it (Fig. 328). Then, using a circular movement, roll underneath the punch, coming back to a standing position on the opposite side of the opponent's arm. In Fig. 329 you can see how to apply a counter-attack at the same time as you roll out of the evasion.

Train this drill in isolation as previously described, then add the defensive elements from the previous training drills.

Fig. 329   Counter-punch to the body.

Fig. 330   Parry the attack.

Fig. 331   Rear parry defence.

Training Drill 8

Parries

The parry is a very simple defence ideally used against a straight punch or possibly even a straight kick, although the risk factor against a kick is considerably higher. For this to work you need a good understanding of speed and timing, as a mistimed parry could result in a punch to the face. The idea of a parry is to knock the attack off-target, causing it to sail past and leave the opponent vulnerable to a counter-attack. For now, we're just going to focus on the defence.

As your partner throws their straight punch, lean the body slightly to the side and, using the nearest hand, strike the attacking hand or arm, knocking the punch off the centreline (Fig. 330). Fig. 331 shows the parry working against a cross punch using the opposite hand to defend with, while Fig. 332 shows the parry working against a rising attack.

Practise defending straight attacks using the parry by isolating defences using each arm for a set amount of time. Refer to the table 'Training Times/Repetitions' at the start of the book for a time guide based on your ability or level.

Once you are confident with this defence, add it to the previous training drills.

Fig. 332   Parry an uppercut.

Fig. 333   Rear-hand stopping defence.

Fig. 334   Lead-hand stopping defence.

Training Drill 9

Stops

A stop is a simple defence that uses timing to halt an attack (namely a circular punch) mid-flow. The targeting point for the stop is the bicep, as it's an easier area to target and is effective enough to take all the energy out of the attack.

To train this defence, instruct a partner to slowly send a hooking punch off their lead arm. As they begin to send the punch, strike the bicep of the attacking arm with a palm strike in order to stop the attack dead (Fig. 333). Even though the attack will be sent slowly to begin with, be sure to keep the guard tight on your opposite side so that you get into the habit of keeping your guard up. A sloppy guard at this stage will always be a sloppy guard, which is the last thing you want when attempting a defence of this nature.

The alternative to this defence is to stop the attack using your lead hand (Fig. 334). Practise each one until you can ideally stop an attack using both the lead and the rear arm, regardless of which hand your opponent is using to attack with.

When confident with this one, try adding it to the other defences.

Training Drill 10

Covering a Kick 1

Covering a kick is slightly different to covering a punch, because the kick is a lot more powerful. In Fig. 335 you see how the knuckles can rest on the cheekbones due to the blocking tool being the forearm this time. This is done because the kick in this instance is a lot lower than the punch in Fig. 320 and any attempt to cover by receiving the kick on the wrists could result in serious injury to the wrist.

If you were to bring the hands higher onto the top of the head as previously shown, the mid-line would be too exposed, increasing the chances of the kick finding its mark.

To train this kick, instruct your partner to send slow and half-power front kicks at you with a steady rhythm. Only really pick up the power and speed with this drill when you are comfortable with it and while wearing protective gear.

Fig. 335   Cover defence against a front kick.

Fig. 336   Cover against a round kick.

Training Drill 11

Covering a Kick 2

This cover shows how to defend against a high-line circular kick, such as a round kick, hook kick or spinning kick. As your opponent kicks, raise your rear-hand guard up so that the hand covers the back of the neck and the lower arm and forearm absorb the energy of the kick.

This defence is effective due to its speed, as the hand moves only very slightly due to the natural position of the rear guard (Fig. 336). To train this drill, instruct your partner to send slow half-power kicks to the head using a steady rhythm, as with training drill 10. Once you become confident, increase the speed and power.

Add this defence to the rest of the drills when you are ready.

Training Drill 12

Lean Back (Against a Kick)

The lean-back defence works well against a kick because it's a very fast natural movement. As the kick comes in, simply lean back out of the way. Keep the lead shoulder high and the rear hand in place as shown in Fig. 337; this will also help to cover you against most possible follow-up attacks.

In order to train this drill, instruct your partner to throw high-level straight and circular kicks while you practise leaning out of their way. Be careful not to lean to the side, as you will run the risk of leaning into an attack if you're not careful. Once your confidence grows with this defence, consider speeding up the attacks then adding it to the previous ones.

Fig. 337   Lean-back defence against a kick.

Training Drill 13

Universal Defence

This is aptly named the universal defence because it is considered to be a defensive move that covers almost any type of kickboxing-style attack. It's a defence that is popular with the light, continuous fighters and predominantly the kicking arts, so we will therefore look at it here.

In order to pull off this defence, you need to adapt your stance into an angled or side-on stance. Then bring your forearms together so that one fist faces the ceiling and the other fist faces the floor. The area that you use to block is then anywhere along the lead arm, with the rear arm alongside for additional support. As you can see from Fig. 338, the defence is an extremely difficult one to get around as everything hides neatly behind it.

Train this defence in the same way as the previous drills, adding to the other defences when you are confident with this one.

Training Drill 14

Evasive Defence

This drill is excellent for practising your ability to evade attacks, while at the same time giving your partner something to aim at that they can actually hit. Place a pair of focus pads on either hand then cross them over, resting the backs of your hands (now in the pads) on the side of the face. From here, instruct your training partner to send half-speed and half-power kicks and punches toward the pads so that you get to practise your evasive manoeuvres using the skills developed in the previous training drills.

In order to avoid getting hit, you must duck, lean, roll, slip and evade all the attacks so that as few as possible land. Train this drill for a set time using the table 'Training Times/Repetitions' at the start of the book as your guide (Fig. 339).

Fig. 338   Universal defence.

Fig. 339   Evasive defence drill.

Fig. 340   Perform a snap punch to the pad.

Training Drill 15

Attack and Defence

All of the drills covered in this chapter so far have focused on receiving an attack. This drill is going to help you get used to instigating the attack, then defending it. It's a great drill to train, as the habit a lot of fighters get into is attacking with a low guard – it's this bad habit that gets a fighter knocked out. If a punch or kick connects on the chin, temple or back of the head, there's a high risk of a knockout. If it connects on the guard, there's less risk of a knockout, as the guard absorbs a great deal of the energy of that attack. A common habit is for the fighter to throw a punch, then let the guard slip or drop. When you receive an attack straight back, as you do in this drill, it will help you get used to keeping that guard tight all of the time.

Snap out a lead jab to the pad (Fig. 340). The instant the jab lands, the pad feeder sends a jab back and you slip the punch (Fig. 341). They then instantly send a cross punch and you slip that punch as well by moving in the opposite direction (Fig. 342). Work this drill for a set time and, once comfortable with it, incorporate footwork and movement from Chapter 8, 'Developing Movement and Footwork'.

Fig. 341   Slip the counter-attack.

Fig. 342   Slip the second counter.

Fig. 343   Jab the pad.

Fig. 344   Retract the punch.

Fig. 345   Jab again.

Training Drill 16

Attack and Defence 2

This drill works the same as training drill 15, except you now add a double jab to initiate the attack (Figs 343 to 345), then receive a double jab back (Figs 346 and 347). As you slip the double jab, try moving the body from left to right or vice versa. This will help with your movement and body mechanics, which are essential for the development of your fighting foundations.

To take this drill even further, after the double slip add a three-punch counter based on your body position after you have slipped the final punch. In this example, a hook, cross, hook would be a natural flowing three-punch counter, as the weight is on the lead foot with the body primed to twist back in again for maximum energy and power (Figs 348 to 350).

Train this drill for a set amount of time and use the table 'Training Times/Repetitions' at the start of the book as a guide based on your current fitness levels.

You can make up your own attack and defence drills using the structure of training drills 15 and 16 as your base. The key thing to get out of the drill is that it's quite common to send an attack in sparring, then immediately receive one back. For this reason, you need to undertake training drills like these, working attacks and defences with counters at the end, as much as possible so that when you spar or fight, your responses will be second nature.

Fig. 346   Slip the jab counter.

Fig. 347   Slip to the other side.

Fig. 348   Send a lead-hook counter.

Fig. 349   Follow with a cross.

Fig. 350   Hook again.

Training Drill 17

Slip and Roll

This drill will help with your movement and body mechanics as well as attacking different levels and angles, all from a simple defensive move. A lot of the time a fighter will limit their movement and attacking angles by not training outside of their comfort zone. While it is comfortable to remain upright and static, it is also very easy to get hit a lot in this position. A good fighter understands that constant movement of the head and body makes them a much harder target to hit.

For this drill, instruct your training partner to place their rear focus pad on your head and hold the lead pad under the arm, as shown in Fig. 351. From here, slip to the inside, keeping the guard tight (Fig. 352), then roll under the arm and uppercut the target pad (Fig. 353), before returning to the start position once more.

Work this drill for a set amount of time, using the table 'Training Times/Repetitions' at the start of the book as your guide.

Fig. 351   Your partner places the pad on your head.

Fig. 352   Slip to the inside.

Fig. 353   Roll underneath and uppercut to the midsection.

Fig. 354   Shin-block a lead-leg round kick.

Fig. 355   Shin-block a rear-leg round kick.

Training Drill 18

Shin Blocks

When training this drill for the first time I would highly recommend that you wear shin pads and footpads, as the bone-on-bone contact from shins clashing is a little too painful for the beginner. You can also add an element of speed and power to the drills and greatly reduce the risk of injury.

A shin block is a very effective blocking tool against a low or, depending on your level of flexibility, even a mid-line kick. It's a very fast defence, as the leg only needs to rise up a little way compared to trying to defend a kick of this nature with your hands or arms. And although you are still actually getting hit when you receive the kick, because the shin connects early on with the kick it's a very good defence, as it takes away the energy of the attack and reduces the overall damage done.

Instruct your partner to aim their round kick at your thigh to begin with. A great deal of the time the kicker will not throw the round kick correctly when anticipating a shin block, so it's important that this is done. As the kick starts its journey, bring your nearest leg straight up so that your shin shields the thigh and absorbs the energy of the kick, stopping it from doing any damage (Fig. 354).

You can also work this drill off your other leg, again blocking with your nearest leg (Fig. 355). It's also possible to block a lead-leg attack using your lead leg and bringing it up and across your body. Try experimenting with the various shin defences against lead- and rear-leg round kicks. When you are confident with them, instruct your training partner to start targeting the mid-line as well.

Work this drill for a set time based on your current level of fitness using the table 'Training Times/Repetitions' at the start of the book as your guide.

Fig. 356   Oblique-kick a lead round kick.

Fig. 357   Oblique-kick a rear round kick.

Training Drill 19

Oblique Kicks

This training drill also works as a defence against a low-level kick, but uses a slightly different defensive technique called an oblique kick. The oblique kick works a little bit like a stamp, therefore when executing the defence you need to move the leg in the same way as if you were about to stamp down on the attacker's leg (as shown in Figs 356 and 357).

The target area for the oblique kick is the knee. However, due to the high risk of injury to your partner if you do connect with the knee, I would strongly suggest aiming a little lower at the shin instead. That way, the most that will happen if you do get a little carried away is a bruised shin, which most people can cope with.

Isolate this training drill initially, then when you feel confident incorporate training drill 18 as well. This will help you get used to various ways of defending against a low-level kick to the thigh.

Training Drill 20

Shuffle-Step Evasion

The next few training drills are going to look at simple defences when receiving kicks. As the kick is quite a powerful weapon to be hit with (some say three times more powerful than a punch), there's no better defence than simply moving out of the way of it. The shuffle-step evasion does just that and uses the opponent's inability to disguise their intentions (telegraphing a technique) to your advantage.

For this drill, your training partner is going to use a side kick to attack with (although in reality it could be any kick as the defence works just the same). With both of you facing each other in a fighting stance (Fig. 358), your partner starts their attack. As they do, shuffle-step back with your lead leg, bringing it back to your rear leg (Fig. 359). At the same time, skip back with your rear leg, increasing the gap between you and your partner (Fig. 360).

As you perform the shuffle step, it is the actual speed of the shuffle movement that clears you out of the way of the attack and the more energy you put into this move, the faster and further back you travel.

Fig. 358   Face your partner.

Fig. 359   Step back with the lead leg.

Fig. 360   Step back with the rear leg.

Training Drill 21

Step-Back Evasion

The step-back evasion is a very fast and simple enhancement of the previous defence. The beauty of learning this drill is that, as a defence, the step-back evasion is very effective at avoiding the kick, while still allowing the opportunity to counter, as you don't move back out of range as you do with the shuffle-step evasion. In your fighting stance (Fig. 361), simply step back with your rear leg as the attack comes in, leaving the front leg where it is (Fig. 362).

Although you can't clearly see the guard position from the photograph, it is advisable to keep a universal guard (training drill 13) in place, just in case the kick still makes contact (which it probably will). From here, if necessary you could spring back up and counter the opponent's attack with relative ease.

Fig. 361   Face your partner.

Fig. 362   Step back with your rear leg.

Training Drill 22

Block and Counter

This block-and-counter drill works by pre-empting the opponent's attack, blocking it in such a way that its energy is removed and thereby rendering it harmless, and striking back at the attacker's 'point of no return' (*see* information box). In this drill, as the attacker throws a round kick to the head of their opponent, the opponent has pre-empted the kick and blocked it. At the same time, they have sent out a counter-punch which catches the attacker on the chin.

This drill works well because you remove the energy from the attack first. In order to do this, you need to move into the attack in order to stop it from building up the energy it needs to do its damage. In this example, the defender actually moves in toward the attack, thereby preventing it from building up any speed and power. At the same time, this forward movement toward the attacker disrupts their balance, making it very difficult to get a second attack out. The counter lands very easily (Fig. 363).

Fig. 363   Move in, cover and counter.

The Point of No Return

The 'point of no return' is the phrase given to the point of the attack at which the fighter is fully committed and therefore unable to stop. For example, in training drill 22, the attacker fully commits to a round kick. The defender anticipates the kick and successfully blocks it. While the attacker has their leg in the air and is therefore vulnerable, the defender launches a counter-strike. In order for the attacker to block the counter-strike with any degree of effectiveness, their kicking leg ideally needs to be back on firm ground. As such, because of their commitment to their original attack, they have reached the point where it is too late to be able to defend the counter successfully due to not being able to recover quickly enough – their point of no return.

Training Drill 23

Drop Evasion

The drop evasion is a particular favourite of mine and is an ideal defence to use when fighting for points, as it is not only fast and effective but once you score a clean point, the fight is stopped, allowing the luxury of full commitment without the risk of a counter-attack from your opponent. It will, however, still work against the continuous fighter, but you will need to ensure that your recovery from this lower position is very quick.

Watch for the tell-tale telegraph of a jab and as soon as you see it, drop the body low, bending from the knees and not the back, and sending a counter jab to the now exposed mid-line (Fig. 364). As you can see from Fig. 364, the body is upright and not bent forward and the guard is in place. This is important, as there is a risk of a lead round kick following the jab once your opponent sees you drop low in this way.

Fig. 364   Drop and counter.

Fig. 365   Defend the first attack.

Training Drill 24

Multiple Attackers

Although not a completely realistic drill to help in fending off multiple attackers, this drill is designed to help with defending an attack that you are turning into. This will ensure you get into the habit of always keeping your guard up, which is a common fault with a lot of fighters.

The pad feeders stand either side, with the defender in the middle facing one pad feeder. The first pad feeder sends out an attack. This can be any random attack to keep the defender on their toes, so to speak, or a nominated one (which may be easier to begin with), and the defender blocks it using a cover (Fig. 365). The defender then immediately sends back either the same technique or a random one based on how the pad is held (Fig. 366).

The defender then turns to face the second pad feeder. The second pad feeder throws any attack at the defender (or a nominated one if preferred) and they defend this using the

Fig. 366   Counter the attack.

Fig. 367   Turn and defend.

Fig. 368   Counter the attack.

appropriate cover (Fig. 367). After defending the attack, the defender sends back an attack of their own to complete the first repetition (Fig. 368).

Continue turning, defending and countering attacks for a set time, using the table 'Training Times/Repetitions' at the start of the book as a guide.

Training Drill 25

Leaning-Back Side Kick

The side kick is probably one of the best defensive kicks available to the kickboxer and this drill will help you to develop this. The key with this defence is speed and timing and having a good understanding of body mechanics. Due to the speed of the attack from your opponent, you won't have time to adjust your body position in order to put you into a favourable stance with which to send the side kick, therefore you need to ensure that when you fight, you are always in that favourable stance and your kicks are loaded and ready to fire.

As you'll see from Fig. 369, the defender is in a short side-on stance. The rear supporting leg is positioned underneath the rear shoulder. This simple positioning of the rear foot allows the lead leg to come off the floor without the need to reposition the rear foot for balance and support, thereby making the kick a lot faster. Normally, fighters stand in long stances that require rear foot movement prior to kicking. This additional movement is enough to slow down an attack (or defence) and telegraph the kick. So the first thing you need to do when practising this drill is to shorten the stance and ensure your lead leg can come off the floor without having to step.

Then as your opponent rushes in to simulate a blitz-style attack, you simply lean back slightly to bring the head away from the attack, transfer your body weight on to your rear leg, and at the same time drive the side kick straight out into the midsection of the attacker (Fig. 370). Practise this drill for a set number of repetitions, making sure you are completely reset in your stance before commencing the next repetition. Use the table 'Training Times/Repetitions' at the front of the book as a guide.

LEFT: Fig. 369 Face the target in a short stance.

RIGHT: Fig. 370 Stop the blitz attack with a side kick.

Training Drill 26

Jumping-Back Side Kick

The jump-back side kick is an excellent variation to the lean-back side kick that you would generally use when the gap between you and your opponent is closed very quickly, such as when they rush at you, catching you unawares. Providing a tight stance is maintained as described above, it should not cause much of a problem, because the necessary distance in order to send that side kick is created by jumping backward. Remember, stepping backward is too slow when defending against a blitz attack of this nature, because you have to step back and then kick. With the jump-back side kick, you simply jump back and kick at the same time, making this defence very fast and very effective.

Set up your stance so that your rear foot is held underneath your rear shoulder and your body weight is distributed with 70 per cent resting on the rear foot, leaving 30 per cent on the lead foot (Fig. 371). Instruct your partner to rush you (or they can do it randomly to simulate realism) and, as they do, jump backward by springing off your rear leg and at the same time drive a side kick into their mid-line (Fig. 372)

LEFT: Fig. 371 Face the target in a short stance.

RIGHT: Fig. 372 Use a jump-back side kick to stop the attack.

Training Drill 27

Jumping-Back Kick

This final variation on the jumping backward style of defensive kicks is probably the most effective one of all. The jumping back kick evolved from a jumping spinning side kick when point fighters realized that in competition the kick was too slow to be effective, so the kick was tweaked by removing part of the spin and making it more of a twist. As such, the spinning back kick and of course the jumping spinning back kick (also known as the jumping back kick) were born.

This kick is not only incredibly fast but probably the most powerful of all the kicks available to the kickboxer and as such it's an extremely effective stopping kick. Not only that but due to the twisting motion, it naturally moves the head and body out of the way of any lead leg attacks your opponent might throw. All in all, this is certainly one to practice.

Stand side on with the rear leg positioned underneath the rear shoulder as before but this time evenly distribute your body weight between both feet (Fig. 373). As soon as your partner steps toward you, jump, twist and drive your rear foot into the midsection using explosive movement (Fig. 374). As you'll note from Fig. 374, the body is actually facing away from the target at the point of impact. This is important as an overspin turns the kick into a side kick which slows the counter down.

Training Drill 28

String Catch

This simple game is very effective, as well as addictive, and is a particular favourite amongst junior students. As such, it is worth introducing into this chapter as it's a great drill for helping you to understand defences and footwork, as well as a great way to introduce a total beginner into the world of free sparring.

Fig. 373   Face the target in a side-on stance.

Fig. 374   Stop the attack with a jumping-back kick.

Fig. 375   Attempt to grab your partner's string.

Fig. 376   Evade your partner's advances.

Fig. 377   The zombie drill evasion.

Start off by tucking a piece of string or thin rope into the front of your trousers. The objective is then to protect that piece of string for as long as you can without your partner stealing it from you. You can use any method of defence, within reason (so no running away or totally covering it with your hands), to prevent your partner from stealing it. Neither of you is allowed to strike the other and all attacks from your partner must be aimed at grabbing the string and nothing else (Fig. 375).

Variations to this drill include:

- swapping the string with your partner each time
- working to a time limit; the person with the smallest number of successful defences does a forfeit
- both fighters wearing a piece of string, with the first person to score ten successful steals winning; loser forfeits as above
- placing the string in the rear of the trousers; this drill helps to develop defensive footwork.

Training Drill 29

Zombie Defence

This drill is aptly named the 'zombie defence' because of the role the attackers play in it. Despite the comical movements of your training partners, their role in this drill will help you to bring together all of the defences, evasions, footwork and movement drills you have been learning in this chapter.

Although you could work this drill with just one training partner playing the role of the zombie, two or more surrounding you will add an element of realism to your movements and defences, as you will need to remain constantly on your toes in order to avoid being touched.

To start the drill, instruct your training partners to stand with their arms outstretched as shown in Fig 376. From here, they simply walk toward you in a slow zombie-like fashion, attempting simply to touch you on a scoring zone (head or body for this drill), while you do everything you can to avoid this happening without obviously turning and running (Figs 376 and 377).

10 Developing Fitness and Stamina

Fitness and stamina are two elements that a fighter has to have in place to ensure that if the fight lasts for more than approximately 30sec, that fighter is capable of continuing. Despite this, a large number of fighters fail to develop their fitness and stamina to a high enough level and, as a result, end up losing the fight due to fatigue.

Fatigue is a really difficult thing to have to deal with, especially if your opponent is fitter and has more stamina. I once had the great pleasure of meeting a martial-arts legend and childhood hero of mine, the great Bill 'Superfoot' Wallace. Bill won the middle-weight world full-contact karate title in 1972 and retired undefeated in 1980 after successfully defending his title twenty-three times. I asked Bill how he trained for his fights and he informed me that a great deal of his training focused on fitness and stamina. Surprisingly, he never trained for the knockout, but was confident enough with his own fitness to know that he could outpace his opponent and win the fight on points. It just so happened that, due to his superior fitness, he actually ended up knocking out a great number of his opponents.

Anyone who has ever taken part in a sporting activity will no doubt have experienced the feeling associated with fatigue at some point in their training. It's the worst place in the world to be and no more so than in the heat of competition. To know you're burnt out and to see your opponent still going is demoralizing in itself and if you're not mentally strong enough to deal with this (see Chapter 14, 'Developing the Mind'), then it could cost you the fight.

There is a saying in the martial-arts world that 'how you train is how you fight' and there is no truer saying. If you train hard, you will fight hard. If you never plan to enter the competitive side of the martial arts, then you may believe that you don't need to worry too much about this chapter and instead simply focus all of your time on the other elements, such as developing that knockout punch. However, it's not just on the mats that you might need to call upon your fitness and stamina. I once trained with an instructor in a street-based fighting system and this instructor's belief was that you should train yourself up to a level where you could survive a three-minute street attack fighting at 100 per cent of your ability. Many of the drills we trained would push us to this limit and it was actually quite an eye-opening experience. It gave those training a new-found respect for the level at which they needed to develop their fitness and stamina.

A good test to see where your fitness and stamina currently sit is to hit a punch bag with full-contact attacks for as long as you can without stopping. I'm fairly confident that there are not many of you out there who could do it for longer than about 60sec without having to stop. If you train hard in the gym, your competitive fights should be easier (not easy – there's a difference). If not, you are doing something wrong.

Fitness and stamina are also often confused. Fitness is all about your body's ability to recover. The faster you recover, the fitter you are. As a fighter, it is standard practice in certain kickboxing bouts to fight for a set amount of time with a given rest period in-between. Although the rest periods are short, ideally you need to be as close to fully recovered as possible before the next round starts. The fitter you are, the closer you will be to starting the next round fully recovered.

Active rest is also something you need to be familiar with, because, realistically, this is the time during a fight when you will have a chance to recover. Active rest is the stage in a fight when you are not attacking. You may be moving around, using your footwork, defending attacks and so on, but your body is working a lot less than it would be if you were constantly attacking. As such, this slight reduction in workload gives the body an opportunity to recover, albeit a bit more slowly. Nevertheless, it all helps and the fitter you are, the faster you body will recover during the active rest stage of a fight.

Stamina, on the other hand, is about how far you can push yourself during the given sporting activity. You often hear stamina associated with running, whereby the more stamina a runner has, the longer they can sustain a higher pace. Stamina, for the kickboxer, helps us to keep fighting (or training) for longer before the body needs to stop for a rest.

When you work through the drills in this chapter it would be worth doing so with a heart-rate monitor in place. During the drills, note to what rate your heart rate increases and how quickly it gets back to a resting rate. The faster it achieves this, the fitter you are. If you make written notes as you train and compare them over a period of weeks, you will be able to deduce whether you are actually getting fitter or not. If you do not have access to a heart-rate monitor, simply take your pulse after finishing a drill and note how long it takes to slow back down to your resting rate once again.

Another suggestion would be to develop your body's ability to recover by introducing an active-rest exercise such as skipping, light jogging, bouncing from foot to foot, shadow sparring and so on in-between drills. Basically, any activity that keeps you working but at a much lower intensity is a great way to develop your ability to recover while still training.

IMPORTANT – Ensure that you have warmed up and stretched correctly before moving on to the following training drills. Use the training guides at the start of the book to assist you.

Training Drill 1

Running

There's probably no greater exercise for developing stamina than running. Running is great for

---

Don't Do Too Much of Everything

I was once privy to a conversation between two martial-arts masters, who shall remain nameless. The first master is a very famous high-level master who spends a great deal of time travelling the world running seminars and making guest appearances. The second master is a well-respected English master who sits at the head of one of the largest martial-arts bodies in the UK. The English master was impressing upon the high-level master what he did to complement his martial-arts training. He explained that on Monday he would run, on Tuesday he would bike, on Wednesday he would swim, on Thursday he would lift weights and so on and gave a very impressive detailed layout (to the uninitiated who were listening in – like myself at the time) of a killer training programme of the very toughest level.

Without batting an eyelid the high-level master asked '... and when do you find the time to fit in your martial-arts training?'

The lesson – train for what you do. If you're a runner, run. If you're a cyclist, cycle. If you're a swimmer, swim. In this day and age, cross-training has become very popular but don't misunderstand these new training methods. By all means run to complement your martial-arts training, but do not let it surpass your actual martial-arts training.

---

conditioning the body and increasing the lungs' ability to take in oxygen. There are two main types of running:

• treadmill running
• road running.

Everyone has a favourite and an opinion on the other. Your objective is to try both and see which you prefer. In the cold, wet, dark winter months I can see how the treadmill could be the favourite; however, when the sun is shining and the sky is blue, it could be the road that you favour. Regardless, I believe that both have their advantages.

I find that the treadmill will push you, as you have to keep up with it. Find a good treadmill with several different training programmes that include incline settings as well as flat run settings. It is worth investing in a good quality machine if you plan on buying one. Ensure it has a high enough speed setting, large enough incline angles and is powerful enough to be able to deal with whoever uses it. Mix up the programmes on a regular basis, otherwise your body gets used to running in a certain way.

Don't just run at a certain speed all the time; try selecting programmes that include *fartlek* (varying speeds and intensity) workouts and sprint work. All this stops the body reaching a plateau and shocks it into continuously developing. Avoid boredom setting in by either listening to music or setting up a TV/DVD player. I watch old fights, the UFC, World Combat League or anything fight-related to keep me motivated when I'm running. Staring at a blank wall as you run is the quickest way to stop you getting back on that treadmill.

Road running gets you out in the fresh air. It's cheap, it can be less boring than a treadmill (if you have nothing to watch), there's a different route each time you run and the natural outdoor terrain will stop the body becoming inert in its development. Always wear a decent pair of running shoes (that you have professionally fitted to match your running style) and undertake a good initial warm-up. Wherever possible, try to run on as many softer surfaces as you can. Grass is an ideal outdoor running surface, as the constant pounding on hard concrete is a sure-fire way to develop running-related injuries.

Finally, don't run before you can walk. Start off slowly and gently, building up over a period of weeks. Above all, use the running to complement your martial-arts training and don't let it overtake it.

Training Drill 2

Skipping

Bruce Lee used to consider skipping to be one of the best exercises, claiming that just 10min of skipping was equivalent to 30min of running.

Although everyone seems to have an opinion on everything nowadays (just look on the Internet for advice on something), who are we to argue with the late, great Bruce Lee?

Skipping is an excellent form of exercise and can be used to develop many different things. As previously mentioned, it's great for active rest, is ideal as a warm-up exercise and is one of the best means of developing stamina available.

Choose a good quality (not necessarily expensive) rope. My favourite is the plain and simple nylon speed rope, but choose one with a bit of weight to it as a lightweight one will be of no use to you, and ensure it is the right size. Ideally, try it out before you buy it. If you stand on the middle of the rope, the handles should reach your armpits. Anything else and the rope's not the right size for you.

Then simply start by hopping on one leg and passing the rope underneath the foot as you bounce, using minimal arm movement. This will take a little practice at first. Continue for a few bounces, then change to the other foot. Keep this

Fig. 378   Use skipping to build your stamina.

bouncing rhythm going for a set time based on your current fitness level. Use the table 'Training Times/Repetitions' at the start of the book as a guide (Fig. 378).

Once you become proficient with this you can try jogging, sprinting (I would recommend 10sec bursts), knee raises, crossovers, a weighted rope and anything else you feel you can master.

Training Drill 3

Conditioning Drills

Conditioning drills are great for strengthening the body and helping to develop overall fitness and stamina. There are a great number of different drills, each with a number of variations. Following is a list of the most popular ones, with some variations to make them even tougher if you want to.

- Push-ups. Be sure to keep the body level throughout the full motion and bring the chest and nose to the floor, avoiding the popular cheat of only lowering halfway down (Fig. 379).
- Crunches. A slight variation on the sit-up that focuses all the tension on the abdominal muscle as opposed to the hips, as with the sit-up. Keep the fingers on the temple and feet off the floor throughout the whole movement (Fig. 380).
- The burpee. One of the best overall body-conditioning exercises that will send your heart rate racing through the roof. Great for developing your stamina (Figs 381 to 383).

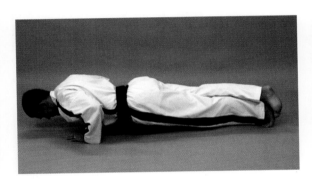

Fig. 379   The push-up.

Fig. 380   The crunch sit-up.

LEFT: Fig. 381   Start position for the burpee.

ABOVE: Fig. 382   Kick the legs back.

RIGHT: Fig. 383   Jump into the air.

Fig. 384　The hyperextension.

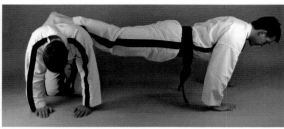

Fig. 385　Rest your feet on your partner's back.

Fig. 386　Perform a push-up.

Fig. 387　Sit on your partner's knees.

Fig. 388　Perform a sit-up.

Fig. 389　Partner-supported hyperextensions.

- The hyperextension. This exercise focuses on the lower back. Simply raise up as high as you can before lowering back down again to the start position (Fig. 384).
- Decline push-ups. A slight spin on the standard push-up that considerably increases your workload and the intensity of the exercise (Figs 385 and 386).
- Supported sit-ups. Find your balance point by sitting on your partner's knees, then lower yourself back while being careful not to go too far, as this would run the risk of injuring the lower back. I would advise going no further than parallel to the floor, as shown in Fig. 388 (Figs 387 and 388).
- Supported hyperextensions. This time your partner sits on the lower legs, preventing the lower body from moving and allowing you to rise further off the floor (Fig. 389).

- Single-leg squats. Supporting yourself on a training partner or other sturdy object, extend a leg out in front, then slowly lower to a squat position before raising back up again (Figs 390 and 391).
- Upright rowing. Grip your partner's hand using an overhand underhand grip. Then move the hands back and forth using a rowing motion in time with your partner. Set different speeds based on what your training partner calls out (for example, one = slow pace, two = medium pace, three = fast pace and so on) (Figs 392 and 393).

There are many ways to train these drills in order to develop fitness and stamina; below are some suggestions.

- As many as you can do in a set time period. Designate an amount of time (for example, 30sec) and do as many of your chosen exercise as you can. Note your score and attempt to beat the previous score on each new attempt. Increase the time when you physically can't do any more in the current time.
- Set a target. Have a set target in mind (for example, twenty) and aim to do twenty of your chosen exercise. Once you can achieve the set target easily, increase it by five.
- Decreasing targets. Aim to hit a set target on your first attempt, then rest for a set amount of time and lower the target by a set number. Repeat for a total of three times (for example, thirty, twenty, ten, with rest periods of 2min after the first set of exercises, followed by 1min after the second set).

Fig. 391   One-legged squats.

Fig. 390   Use your partner for support.

Fig. 392   Start position for upright rowing.

LEFT: Fig. 393   End position for upright rowing.

Suggested Kikbo Exercises

1 = jab	2 = front kick	3 = push-up
4 = cross	5 = round kick	6 = sit-up
7 = backfist strike	8 = side kick	9 = hyperextension
10 = jab & cross	11 = knee strike	12 = burpee
13 = elbow strike	14 = hook kick	15 = cat dip
16 = lead & rear hooks	17 = axe kick	18 = leg raise
19 = lead & rear uppercuts	20 = bodyweight squats	

- Incorporate a series of exercises into a circuit (*see* above, training drill 3)

Training Drill 3

Kikbo

Kikbo is a kickboxing circuit training session that we developed at our kickboxing schools. It is designed to take you through a gruelling cardio workout to help develop your stamina and increase your fitness, with an element of mental training thrown in.

Designate twenty stations to use in the circuit. Try to incorporate one hand, followed by one leg, followed by one exercise. See the table for a suggestion of exercises to use.

You can either work everything on your own using a punch bag, or you can work with a training partner and alternate holding pads for each other, which will give you a much longer rest period. If working with a partner, the table below provides some suggestions for exercises.

Ideal training lengths for this drill are 1min, with 30sec rest in-between. In that time, aim to do as many of each of the designated techniques as possible, followed by the rest period. As you

can see, this drill will not only push you to your max, but will also condition the body to recover as quickly as possible before the next round begins. Because of the intensity of this drill, I would suggest training it no more than once a week.

My suggestion would also be to train with a heart-rate monitor. Note your heart-rate maximum and minimum scores and also keep a score of the number of exercises you manage to do. That way, you have a target to beat the next time you attempt the drill.

Training Drill 4

Seated Round Kicks

The next few drills are not only going to develop fitness and stamina, but will also aid toward a little body conditioning at the same time. Although we are going to use the next few seated kicks as a training drill, kicking from the ground in this way is actually a very effective street application should you ever find yourself in a situation where you are on the ground and your opponent is standing in front of you. As such, it's certainly worthwhile striking the pad with 100 per cent

Suggested Kikbo Exercises with a Partner

1 = jab & cross	2 = jab & cross	3 = front kicks
4 = front kicks	5 = push-ups	6 = lead & rear hooks
7 = lead & rear hooks	8 = round kicks	9 = round kicks
10 = sit-ups	11 = lead & rear uppercuts	12 = lead & rear uppercuts
13 = side kicks	14 = side kicks	15 = hyperextensions
16 = elbow strikes	17 = elbow strikes	18 = knee strikes
19 = knee strikes	20 = burpees	

Fig. 394   From a seated position.

Fig. 395   Perform seated round kicks.

power so that you also develop this key element at the same time.

In a seated position with your pad holder standing side on (Fig. 394), raise yourself up using your forward leg and rear arm as a support and, by turning your body into the kick shield as you kick, aim to strike the pad as fast and hard as you can (Fig. 395). Bounce the leg off the kick shield (this will actually happen naturally, so just control the leg back to the floor) and immediately spring back up again to strike once more.

My suggestion would be initially to aim to strike the pad a set number of times. Because these types of drills are quite demanding, setting a time duration may actually be too much to begin with. Once you can achieve your set number of repetitions with ease, consider training to a time limit instead.

Training Drill 5

Seated Side Kicks

This training drill works in exactly the same way as the previous one, except that you now hit the pad with a side kick. In order for this to work, your training partner needs to stand front on and you

now kick with your forward leg. If your balance is good, you can support yourself using one hand; otherwise, you might want to consider using both hands to support yourself until your balance improves. Figs 396 and 397 show this drill in action.

Fig. 396   From a seated position.

Fig. 397   Perform seated side kicks.

Fig. 398   From a seated position.

your non-kicking leg. As you do, chamber the kicking leg in readiness for the back kick (Fig. 399). Strike the target (Fig. 400) and as you bounce the leg off the pad, return to a seated position once more by reversing your movement before starting the next kick.

Fig. 399   Spin backward.

Training Drill 6

Seated Back Kicks

As before, except this time strike the pad with a spinning back kick from a seated position. Facing the kick shield front on (Fig. 398), spin around so that you support yourself using both hands and

Fig. 400   Perform a seated back kick.

Training Drill 7

Push-Up Kicks

This particular drill is extremely tough, but with regular practice it will over time develop your stamina and fitness to new levels. Due to its intensity, it would be advisable not to attempt this drill until you can perform the previous ones well. For those of you who are ready for the challenge, however, here's how it works.

Start from a push-up position with your pad feeder holding a kick shield side on as shown in Fig. 401. Perform a push-up and, as you push yourself back up, spring up, driving your leg through and transitioning into a seated position (this needs to be done explosively in order to set up the seated position correctly) (Fig. 402). From the seated position, perform the kick in the normal way (Fig. 403) and return to the seated position. From here, you need to spring back into a push-up position by reversing the jumping motion you previously did. Once back into your push-up position, start the process again for the second repetition.

Fig. 401   From a push-up position.

Fig. 402   Jump into a seated position.

Fig. 403   Perform a seated round kick.

Training Drill 8

Seated Spinning Kicks

This final seated kicking drill is unfortunately going to throw your equilibrium all over the place, so for that reason it is advisable to try to pace yourself, setting up a steady and deliberate rhythm as you kick and spin. From a seated posi- tion (Fig. 404), spin around so that you support yourself on your non-kicking leg and both hands (Fig. 405). Continue the spin and as you come back round toward the target, once again drive the rear leg into the pad as hard as you can (Fig. 406). From here, immediately reverse the spin so that you return to your seated position once more before starting the next kick.

Fig. 404   From a seated position.

Fig. 405   Spin backward.

Fig. 406   Perform a seated spinning kick.

Training Drill 9

Power Punches 1

This training drill can either be done on your own using a punch bag, or with a training partner holding a pair of focus pads or possibly even a kick shield. For manoeuvrability focus pads would be the obvious choice, but the kick shield is a great training aid for power attacks. Regard- less of your current fitness levels, set the timer for 2min, then ensure you punch the pads as hard as you can for every punch. As you'll know from Chapter 4, 'Developing Power', when attacking the pads full-contact, it is necessary to slow each attack down and make each punch solid and deliberate, so that in a four-punch combination you take a second to perform each punch and not a second to perform all four punches.

As soon as the timer goes off, drop down and do ten push-ups, ten sit-ups and ten burpees, before resting. Wearing a heart-rate monitor here would be useful as you can then start the next round when your heart rate reaches a certain level. A rough guide would be to aim to start the next round at around 120bpm. Alternatively, you can simply rest for a minute or, if working with a partner, you get to rest while holding the pads for them.

Training Drill 10

Power Kicks 1

This training drill works along the same lines as the previous one, except with kicks instead of punches. Again, when working with a training partner you can use focus pads for manoeuvrability or kick shields if your kicks are particularly powerful. Alternatively, if you are training alone a punch bag is an ideal training aid.

A variation on training drills 9 and 10 would be to alternate each drill. For example, on the first round only use punches followed by ten of each exercise, then on the second round, isolate your kicks followed by ten of each. You can even add a third round and mix up both hands and legs, followed by ten of each exercise.

Training Drill 11

30-Second Fitness Blast

This is perhaps one of the best training drills for developing fitness, as it is designed to do just that and progression and development can be clearly seen. Choose six exercises that vary the body parts used, for example:

- star jumps
- push-ups
- sit-ups
- burpees
- hyperextensions
- cat dips.

The exercises can be changed to suit. Starting with the first exercise, aim to perform as many repetitions as you can within 30sec. Once the timer goes off, rest for 30sec before starting the next exercise. Complete each exercise using the 30sec on/30sec off principle.

Ideally, make a note of the number of repetitions you do of each exercise so that you can aim to beat it when you next do the drill. As your fitness levels improve, you will reach a stage where you can't physically beat your best score. When this happens, increase the time by 15sec. Train with a heart-rate monitor on if you have one, making a note of your heart rate at the beginning and end of each exercise. The lower these are, the fitter you are becoming.

Training Drill 12

Two-Pad Kicking Drill

This drill ideally requires two pad holders (holding kick shields), or two punch bags positioned either side of you. To perform the drill, kick each pad in turn as fast as possible for a set amount of time. Nominate a particular kick (I would suggest sticking with the basic kicks, such as front kick, round kick and side kick) and aim to hit the pads as many times as you can with that kick.

Variations on this drill would be either to kick the pads using the same leg each time (for example, if you chose the round kick, you would kick the first pad with your left leg, then turn into a right lead and kick the opposite pad with the same leg again). Or you could kick with the opposite leg (for example, with your right leg in front, you would kick the first pad with the left leg, then turn to the other pad, ensuring that you spin into a left lead and kick the second pad with your right leg). Just make sure that the pad feeders are standing the correct way round before you start (Figs 407 and 408).

Training Drill 13

High-Rep Kicking Drill

This is a simple short and sharp drill that involves sudden explosive bursts of energy combined with short rest periods. Nominate an explosive kick such as a round kick or a side kick and perform ten as fast as you can, one after the other. Ideally with this type of kick, you want to kick off your

Fig. 407   Kick the first kick shield.

Fig. 408   Turn and kick the second kick shield.

lead leg and bounce the foot off the floor to assist with the speed. Back leg kicks would be too slow for this drill.

As soon as you have done ten kicks, swap the pads with your training partner, resting while they perform their kicks. Continue kicking and swapping the pads for a set amount of time (Figs 409 to 411).

Add an element of competition to this drill by issuing a forfeit to whoever is still kicking when the timer runs out.

Training Drill 14

Circle of Fitness

This is a great training drill when there's a group of you training together. The group forms a circle facing each other (Fig. 412), then each person nominates an exercise. Ideally, people should nominate exercises that will work particular body parts in order and not the same ones straight after each other (for example, don't do crunches followed by sit-ups). Then, working round the circle, each person takes it in turn to set the pace by counting out loud from one to ten while everyone (including the counter) performs a repetition to each count (Fig. 413).

When you complete each exercise, move straight onto the next one without resting. When all of the exercises are finished, go straight back to the first one and repeat the drill without resting. If possible, three full circuits of all the exercises should be completed before stopping.

Fig. 409   Kick the kick shield.

Fig. 410   Bounce the foot off the floor.

Fig. 411   Kick the kick shield again.

Fig. 412   Working in a circle.

Fig. 413   Perform a set of exercises together.

Training Drill 15

Power Punches 2

Follow the same principle as that for training drill 9 (power punches 1), except this time strike the pads for a total of 3min before stopping for a rest. Due to the extra amount of time, the exercises have been omitted from this drill. Once the 3min timer has gone off, rest for a minute before moving on to the next training drill, or repeat this drill once more.

Training Drill 16

Power Kicks 2

As above, but using kicks instead of punches.

Training Drill 17

Ten and Switch

This is another training drill that ideally works with two other training partners, or one and a punch bag. The latter will give you more of a workout, with the former providing more rest. Choose a technique; this can actually be anything you want, as every technique lends itself to this training drill. The objective is to perform the technique ten times and as fast as possible. While you do this, your training partner performs a chosen exercise for as long as it takes you to do the ten techniques. You then switch places. If there are three of you working together, move from puncher, to pad feeder, to exercises in that order.

Perform this drill for a set amount of time, then change the technique and exercise. Work the drill for a total of five techniques before changing the drill (Fig. 414).

Training Drill 18

High, Middle, Low

This training drill is not only going to develop your stamina, it will also condition the legs because of the constant changing of levels. Starting with a jab, cross-combination, strike the pads in an upright position. Then, immediately drop to kneeling and jab, cross again. From here, drop into a seated position and perform another jab, cross. Finally, lie on your back and perform a jab, cross again. Then jump straight back up to standing and repeat the whole drill a second time.

A variation on this drill is to work your way back up to standing by transitioning back through the levels instead of simply standing back up again. For example, from the lying position, transition back to seated and perform a jab, cross. Then kneel and perform a jab, cross, then stand and perform a jab, cross.

Try working your defences alongside this drill by not using your hands to help you transition between the levels. You can instruct your pad feeder to attack as you change levels, so as to help you practise your covers and rely solely on your balance and leg strength to stand back up again. Figs 415 to 418 show this drill in action.

Training Drill 19

Leg Grab

This final drill is quite a fun one and adds an element of competition to developing your fitness and stamina. Wherever possible, adding an element of competition to your drills will not only

Fig. 414   One pad feeder, one puncher and one doing the exercises.

Fig. 415   Punch the pad high section.

Fig. 416   Punch the pad mid-section.

Fig. 417   Punch the pad low section.

Fig. 418   Punch the pad on the ground.

make them more enjoyable, but will also encourage you to push yourself harder than you might otherwise have done.

With this drill, you compete against your partner, attempting to grab and lift one of their legs off the floor. They naturally have to prevent you from achieving this, but it is to be done by staying within the parameters decided at the start of the drill (for example, no turning around, no running away, no striking and so on). At the same time, they have to grab and lift one of your legs off the floor.

You can either work this drill for a set amount of time or for a set number of leg lifts. Nominate a forfeit for the person who achieves the smallest number of leg lifts (Fig. 419)

Fig. 419   Attempt to grab your partner's leg.

11 Developing Sparring

If you have followed the training drills and chapters of the book in order, by this point you should be ready to put all of the elements together and this is ultimately where sparring comes in. Sparring is the element that brings all your training and all the key elements we've looked at so far together and helps you take your martial-arts training to the next level. It is, without question, an essential element that anyone serious about their martial-arts training really shouldn't be without.

If your sole intention of studying the martial arts is simply to lose weight, get fit, improve your flexibility and so on, then training in a fighting art such as kickboxing will certainly help you to achieve these things (providing you train properly, of course). However, the only way to improve your sparring or fighting ability is actually to spar or fight (sparring is the development of your fighting skills under controlled conditions with a training partner, whereas fighting is testing your skills in competition, or in an environment in which the intensity and pressure are increased, often referred to as 'pressure testing').

To neglect this key element of your training is like learning to drive a car by simply sitting in it and going through the motions, but never actually taking it for a drive. Only when you take it for a drive do you fully understand how so many additional factors affect your performance behind the wheel. If you spent the first four years of your training (the length of time it takes on average to achieve a black belt in kickboxing) simply punching pads, then decided to try sparring with someone who had only half the time you had in the martial arts but had spent their years sparring, the chances are they would be a great deal more rounded, certainly more experienced and more than capable of beating you competitively.

Competition categories include sections such as forms (also known as kata or patterns), musical forms, fighting, breaking (or destruction) and weapons, to name but a few. The forms competitor, for example, normally has incredible technical ability with amazing flexibility and understands body mechanics to a very high level. The fighter, however, does not necessarily need to have the same skill sets as the forms competitor, because their side kick does not need to be technically perfect, as no one is judging that aspect. They just need to be able to hit their opponent with it, regardless of how sloppy it may actually look. If it scores a point, who cares? As such, a fighter entering a forms competition is unlikely to win because of these factors and the same is true for a forms competitor entering a point-sparring bout. Although technically more superior, the forms competitor does not need to develop their defences, movement or footwork to the same degree as the fighter, as no one ever attacks them. In competitive martial arts, you often see high-level martial artists specializing in certain divisions and rarely do they cross over.

Consequently, you can have a long and prosperous journey in the martial arts without ever actually needing to enter the world of sparring. However, if you really want to understand what all the training in the martial arts can do for you, and how this once battlefield art form is ultimately designed to make a fighter out of you, then be sure to spend a little time studying the training drills and sparring techniques in this chapter.

IMPORTANT – Ensure that you have warmed up and stretched correctly before moving on to the following training drills. Use the training guides at the start of the book to assist you. You will also require a full complement of sparring

Fig. 420   Keeping one leg off the floor.

Fig. 421   Use this leg to attack with.

safety equipment for this section, comprising a headguard, boxing gloves (or similar), gum shield, groin guard, shin pads and foot pads.

Training Drill 1

One-Legged Kicking

This fun drill is designed to help you develop your balance and leg strength as well as your kicking ability, while giving your partner a chance to develop their defensive ability. You start off facing each other in your preferred fighting stance and the attacker lifts their kicking leg off the floor (Fig. 420). From this position, the attacker can only kick using the leg that is in the air and they must not put that foot down. Naturally, they can send either single or multiple kicks toward the opponent and use either continuous or broken rhythm to attack with.

The defender cannot move and must stand their ground and defend or evade every attack that is thrown at them. The attacker has full movement capabilities providing they do not put their foot on the floor (Fig. 421).

You can work this drill in several ways. Either work to a time limit, for example 1min, then swap

roles, or swap roles when the attacker puts their foot down or drops their knee below a certain point.

Training Drill 2

One-Legged Boxing

This drill works along similar lines to the previous drill, but with two major differences. You now replace the kicks with punching techniques and you both hold a leg in the air. You can also now both move around attacking and defending at the same time (Fig. 422).

There are several ways in which you can train this drill. Initially start off accumulating points each time you land a clean punch to a scoring zone. Then, after a set time limit of your choosing, the fighter with the lowest score gets a forfeit.

Alternatively, each time someone puts a foot down during a bout they receive a forfeit. The forfeits can increase in intensity each time (for example, start off with five push-ups and increase by five each time). Finally, set a maximum score (for example, ten points) and the first person to achieve this score wins the round. The loser does a forfeit.

Fig. 422   One-legged boxing drill.

Training Drill 3

One-Legged Sparring

This drill completes the 'one-legged' series by introducing the final stage of this kind of training

drill. For this one, you both stand with one leg in the air and you can both attack and defend using any technique and defence manoeuvre. Use the same variations as described in the last two training drills if you want to make the drill different in any way (Figs 423 and 424).

Training Drill 4

Wall Sparring

If you have never experienced wall sparring, this is a sparring drill you really should not be without. It not only limits your fighting range, but is a great drill for helping you to develop your defensive ability due to the restriction it sets on your movement. Anyone who fights in an environment where they may run out of space (such as in a boxing ring or cage), will benefit greatly from this training drill.

To begin with, stand with your back against a wall. From here, your partner sends their attacks at you; you need to reduce the number of techniques that hit you by using your defence and evasions skills while remaining stationary (Fig. 425).

You can add several variations to this drill by isolating attacks only (for example, all you can do

Fig. 423   Both fighters keep a leg off the floor.

Fig. 424   Attack using only that leg.

Fig. 425   Wall-sparring drill.

Fig. 426   Back-to-back sparring drill.

is defend), or you can both attack and defend but naturally the defender must keep their back against the wall at all times. You can also isolate the attacks using hands only, legs only, or you can attack with both.

Work these drills to a set time limit based on your level of fitness.

One tip regarding this drill is actually to stand with the heel of your rear foot against the wall as opposed to your back. What this will do is allow you a greater range of upper body movement with which to work your evasions, while still restricting your overall manoeuvrability.

Training Drill 5

Back-to-Back Sparring

This drill works along similar lines to the previous one, except this time you are going to have your back against your training partner's back instead of the wall. Now you can both move around, providing you keep your backs together throughout the drill. At the same time, you both face an opponent who can move both forward and back to enter and exit the fighting ranges in order to set up their attacks.

As you will see from this drill, your movement is still very restricted and as such you are going to have to rely on your ability to defend in order to minimize the damage that you take. Providing you work as a team, you can move around in order to close and increase the gap between you and your opponents, but you cannot break away from each other at any point.

Work this for a set time limit and then swap roles. You can also isolate hands only, legs only and hands and legs to add variation to the drill (Fig. 426).

Training Drill 6

Close Sparring

Close sparring simulates the fighting situation you can often find yourself in when you and your opponent manage to close the distance between you to such an extent that you are now physically touching one another. This is possibly the most difficult range to fight in, particularly if takedowns are not permitted in your fighting style. Within this close-range proximity it is not only difficult to throw techniques (and nearly impossible to throw kicks), but it can also be a very dangerous area to be in as it is quite likely that your opponent will be throwing hooks and uppercuts (and elbows if permitted) and it is generally these types of punches that are excellent finishing techniques.

In your preferred fighting stance (you may well find that a front-on stance works better for this drill), stand next to your partner so that your lead

Fig. 427   Close-range sparring drill.

shoulders are touching. Then for a set amount of time you both attack and defend, trying to land as many attacks as possible, while also attempting to reduce the number of attacks that land (Fig. 427).

Training Drill 7

Same Technique

This simple drill is really good for developing an explosive attacking ability using a set technique only. Similar to working a technique in isolation on a punch bag or pair of focus pads, the constant repetition used in this drill will help to enhance your technical fighting ability and improve the success rate of using isolated or single technique attacks while sparring or when in competition.

With your sparring partner, chose a technique that you are both happy to use and while sparring in the normal way, only use this nominated technique to attack with.

Work this drill for a set time, based on your levels of fitness.

Training Drill 8

Different Technique

This drill works in exactly the same way as the previous one, except that you now choose a different technique to your sparring partner. Again, isolate only one technique and use that technique to spar against your partner, who also uses one isolated technique (you use a jab and your partner uses a cross, for example).

Training Drill 9

One Hand and One Leg

This time, you isolate the one-hand technique, while your partner isolates the one-leg technique. You both spar together for a set period of time using your chosen hand and leg techniques. On the second round, you swap around (so you now use legs and your partner uses hands) and choose different hand and leg techniques to the previous round. Continue sparring in this way for a set number of rounds.

Training Drill 10

Just Hands

In order to develop your punching ability when sparring, you need to spend some time only using your hands. With this drill, you do just that. Set a time limit and a chosen number of rounds that you can both work to and start sparring, using hands only. Be sure to incorporate all of the elements you have covered so far such as footwork, movement, speed, timing and defences.

Training Drill 11

Just Legs

As delivering a successful kick is somewhat harder than delivering a successful punch, some stand-up fighters of kicking arts tend not to include them when they spar. To do so, in my opinion, is to limit yourself considerably and is not dissimilar to laying down many of your most useful weapons, because you have not taken the time to learn how to use them.

Punches work great at a certain fighting range, but outside of this range the kicker is king. Not only that, but certain kicks are designed to attack at certain angles and, as such, mastering your kicking ability when sparring will almost certainly double your fighting power.

Work this drill in the same way as the previous one.

Training Drill 12

Single Technique

This drill can be done in two separate ways. Either you both spar using single techniques only (for example, you can only attack with a single technique as opposed to using multiple techniques and combinations), or your sparring partner attacks in the normal way and you can only use single techniques.

This drill will help you to develop your explosive attacking ability as well as your counter-fighting ability, as most counter-punches are based on single attacking techniques.

Work this drill for a set period of time.

Training Drill 13

Combination Sparring

For this final drill in the series you and your sparring partner decide upon a set combination, for example jab, cross, lead-leg round kick. As you spar, you can only use this combination in the exact order that you have set, but how you use this is up to you. For example, you can send the combination together (for example, jab, cross and lead-leg round kick), or you can send the combination with broken rhythm (for example, jab, pause, cross and lead-leg round kick, or jab, cross, pause, lead-leg round kick and so on). This way, your opponent can never pre-empt your attack and be ready to block or evade before the technique is thrown.

A slight variation on this drill is to choose a different combination to your sparring partner. Work this drill for a set period of time before changing the combination.

Training Drill 14

Circular Movement

This is a great training drill for helping to develop your footwork while sparring. Footwork is a key element of a fight and having the ability quickly

Fig. 428   Face your partner.

Fig. 429   Use circular movements to avoid being hit.

Points are irrelevant for this game, as every clean point finishes the fight regardless. Two fighters fight off and the first one to score a clean point wins the round. The winner then stays on and the loser moves off to join the back of the queue ready for another turn. If training with just one partner, every time a clean attack is scored the other person does a forfeit.

Continue for a set amount of time, then for the final round announce that when a fighter loses from this point onward, they are out of the game. The last fighter left in is the overall winner. Add an element of additional competition by issuing a forfeit each time someone goes out.

When scoring, ensure that the winner is clearly defined by raising a hand toward the fighter who scored the point (Fig. 430).

to switch direction and move or side-step out of the way of an attack is a great skill. Start off facing your sparring partner in your favourite stance (Fig. 428). Then by pivoting on your lead leg only, your objective is to keep moving either left or right (clockwise or anti-clockwise) in order to prevent your partner from landing a clean attack.

The attacker can move in any direction and in any way and must attempt to land a clean attack whenever they see an opening while you pivot, defend and counter their attacks (Fig. 429).

Training Drill 15

'Killer'

This is a great fun game that adds an element of competition to your training and helps to develop your competitive fighting ability. The larger the group, the better, although you can actually work with just one sparring partner using a great element of fairness, honesty and trust. Alternatively, you will need a referee and as many fighters as possible. The referee controls the fighting and does not actually fight, although the game can be adapted so that each person who loses moves into the role of the referee for one fight.

Fig. 430   'Killer' competitive fighting drill.

Training Drill 16

Half-Speed

This simple drill is ideally designed to work your defences and evasions as you send your attacks at half-speed. Working with your sparring partner, you can choose to isolate techniques, combinations or hand and leg attacks and send all of your techniques using half-speed and power. This slower attacking speed will give you and your training partner a greater chance to see the attacks coming and a much better opportunity to defend against them.

Work this drill for a set amount of time based on your levels of fitness

Training Drill 17

Hand Slap

This is a simple training drill for developing hand and eye coordination as well as timing and explosive speed. Facing your sparring partner in a fighting stance, your objective here is to attack the chest area with a specific single-hand technique. As you attack, your partner's objective is to prevent the attack from landing by simply defending the attack using blocks, covers and parries only. They are not allowed to move out of the way or step back (Fig. 431).

You can either work this training drill for a set period of time and both maintain the same roles, swapping once the time is up, or you can alternate the attacks one for one. You can also add an element of competition by keeping a score of how many times you make a successful hit. The person with the lowest score at the end does a forfeit.

Training Drill 18

Foot Slap

This drill adds a slight spin on the previous one, as your objective now is to try to kick your partner on the belt line (exercise control for this drill so that you reduce the risk of injuring your partner accidentally), while they try to defend against your attack. As before, the defence can include parries, covers and blocks, but not movement

Fig. 431   Hand-slap drill.

Fig. 432   Foot-slap drill.

and footwork. That way, you get to practise your defences (Fig. 432).

As before, add an element of competition by keeping score of the points accumulated and issue a forfeit to the person who scores the least at the end of the rounds. Either work to a time limit and then either switch roles, or work one for one, swapping between attacker and defender at each turn.

Training Drill 19

Non-Contact Sparring

Non-contact sparring is the starting point for anyone who is interested in starting to develop their sparring skills. It is by far the safest and most injury-free option and, as such, is an ideal starting point for the beginner (although, to be honest, statistically the risk of injury while train-

ing is far greater in other sports such as football than it is in the martial arts). For the experienced martial artist, non-contact sparring is a great warm-up drill prior to commencing actual sparring.

In order to spar 'non-contact', attack in exactly the same way as you would if making contact, except that all of your techniques must be pulled short of your partner so that none actually land. At the same time, your partner goes through the motions of defending each attack in order to get used to this side of sparring, safe in the knowledge that nothing is actually going to hit them (Figs 433 and 434).

You can choose to isolate specific attacking techniques such as hands only, legs only, one attacks, one defends and so on. Work each non-contact sparring bout for a time duration based on your fitness levels.

Fig. 433   Non-contact sparring using legs.

Fig. 434   Non-contact sparring using hands.

Training Drill 20

Two-on-One Sparring

Two-on-one sparring is a great drill to help you understand what it is like to be in a multiple-attack situation. Although in actual sparring you rarely, if ever, have to fight against multiple attackers, this drill is not only going to heighten your awareness, but it will also raise your sparring ability to the next level. After all, if you can fight against two opponents, one is going to be so much easier.

To start with, place yourself between your two attackers. Then, for a set period of time based on your level of fitness, attack and defend against multiple attackers, ideally aiming to use your footwork and defensive skills to minimize the number of hits you take, while at the same time aiming to land as many successful attacks on your opponents as you can (Fig. 435).

The best advice I can give to help you 'survive' this scenario is to avoid fighting two opponents at the same time. Instead, aim to place one attacker in-between you and the second attacker so that you use the attacker nearest to you as a natural shield against the second one. You will have to use your footwork in order to achieve this, but it will mean that you are only ever fighting one attacker at a time.

Fig. 435   Two-on-one sparring drill.

12 Developing Shadowing

Shadow sparring, or shadowing as it is also known, is the practice of performing your kicks, punches and defensive skills against an imaginary opponent or opponents. It is also a key attribute of all good fighters and having an ability to shadow spar well significantly helps in the development of fighting skills. Unfortunately, shadow sparring is not always practised amongst all the martial-arts styles and as such it is normally only really associated with fighting styles such as boxing or kickboxing (and then not in every kickboxing school). The truth is that any martial-arts form can incorporate shadow sparring into its training curriculum regardless of whether that particular form focuses on stand-up or ground fighting. If not, there is nothing stopping the individual from incorporating it into their private training sessions.

To be able to move around, using footwork and movement, attack an imaginary opponent using kicks and punches and defend against imaginary attacks, actually takes great skill. At first, it will seem quite unnatural and it is for this reason that many people tend to steer away from shadow sparring. However, as shadow sparring is a skill, perseverance is the key and, as with all skills, this attitude together with a steadfast determination will help you to develop your shadow-sparring ability and take your training to the next level.

This chapter will focus on training drills to help you to understand fully what's involved when shadow sparring and will teach you how to shadow spar well. We will incorporate simple drills that you can work on your own or with a training partner to help get you started and to help you understand how to take your shadow sparring to the next level. Once you have completed this chapter, you can use the skills that you develop here to complement your existing training drills, or to help you to develop specific training drills such as the enhancement of a certain drill, technique or combination.

Shadowing a new technique over and over again, for example, is a great way of locking it into the nervous system (the part of the body responsible for conditioned responses that are developed through constant repetition), so that it becomes a natural movement when you need to call on it. Failure to lock something into the nervous system in this way will be the reason it lets you down when you come to use it. It is said that you need to practise something more than 2,000 times before it becomes locked in.

So try not to think of shadow sparring as a way of just developing your sparring ability, but instead use this new-found skill to help you to develop any aspect of your martial-arts training that you need to focus on, particularly when you don't have a training partner to help you.

IMPORTANT – Ensure that you have warmed up and stretched correctly before moving on to the following training drills. Use the training guides at the start of the book to assist you.

Training Drill 1

Footwork

To commence your journey into the world of shadow sparring, start off by simply practising your footwork drills. With reference to the training you undertook in Chapter 8, 'Developing Movement and Footwork', simply move around in your fighting stance using your footwork skills (Figs 436 and 437). Be sure to include forward and backward movement, side steps, defensive steps covering distance and creating distance,

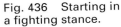

Fig. 436 Starting in a fighting stance.

Fig. 437 Move around using your footwork.

start a new round, increase the drill by 10sec resting, for the same amount of time (for example, in the second round you increase the drill to 20sec, with 20sec rest, third round 30sec and so on).

I would also suggest that you shadow spar using 100 per cent energy, as opposed to a reduction in your energy levels. This will be quite hardgoing, but it will not only improve your fitness levels, it will also get you into the habit of training at full speed, which is another reason for starting off at just 10sec and incorporating adequate rest periods into the drill.

Training Drill 2

Add in Single Techniques

You can either add this training drill into the previous one, or work it as a separate entity. My advice is to build up the initial drill by adding in the following drills either after each rest period, or after a set period of time (for example, build up the first one to a full minute, then start back at 10sec but adding in this drill as well). This time, continue shadowing your footwork, but now start adding in single attacking techniques. These can be kicks or punches as well as elbows or knees (Fig. 438 and 439).

and treat the whole exercise as if you were sparring or fighting an imaginary opponent.

Regardless of your fitness levels, my advice when developing your shadow-sparring ability for the first time is to start off by shadowing for just 10sec, then rest for 10sec and start again. Each time you

Fig. 438 Add in punches to your shadowing.

Fig. 439 Add in kicks to your shadowing.

Work this new drill in the same way as the previous one by building up the drill using 10sec increments as before.

Training Drill 3

Add in Combinations

Now it's time to build up your attacks by incorporating multiple attacks into your shadow sparring. You can either free-play these, adding any number of combinations you like, or you can choose to nominate a set combination (or combinations) and only use these. For example, you may choose to use a jab, cross and lead-leg round kick combination. If so, as you are moving around using your footwork and throwing single techniques, every now and again explode with a combination of attacks before resetting and continuing with your footwork once more. Remember your footwork is also an opportunity for you to recover, much like when you actually spar (remember the section on active rest in Chapter 10, 'Developing Fitness and Stamina') – you burn out when you attack and recover when you move and defend.

As before, start off working for 10sec and build up to 1min (or longer if you wish) in 10sec increments.

Fig. 440   Add in defences to your shadowing.

Training Drill 4

Add in Defences

This is the final stage in the development of your basic shadow-sparring skills. Now you can add in the defences. As you move around using your footwork and sending out single and multiple attacks, you are also going to imagine that you are receiving attacks from an opponent and consequently you need to defend each imaginary attack accordingly. Practise shadowing your covers, movement and evasions as well as your blocks and parries, using all of the defences incorporated in Chapter 9, 'Developing the Defences' (Fig. 440).

This essential stage in your shadow-sparring development is one that many fighters, even though they incorporate shadow sparring into their training, miss out. Over time, breaking each stage down in this way will be unnecessary, but for now it will help you a great deal. Be sure to incorporate all the aspects of the drills covered so far to ensure you are getting the maximum benefit out of your shadow-sparring training.

Work this final stage of shadow sparring using the same timing sets as before.

Training Drill 5

Move Around

For this drill, you will need the help of a training partner, or an audio training CD if a training partner is unavailable (I just so happen to have one available on my website www.fightingstuff .com that will do the job). Move around as you have been doing in the previous shadow-sparring drills, focusing on your footwork, attacks and defences. However, this time when your training partner calls out a technique you explode with that technique as fast as possible before continuing with your shadow sparring.

Instruct your training partner randomly to call out attacks using a broken rhythm technique so that you don't become used to a certain rhythm. The explosion needs to be as random and as sudden as possible. Once you become used to this, your training partner can also start calling out combinations of techniques.

A variation on this drill is to number each technique or combination of techniques so that your partner calls out the number instead of the names of the techniques. This will make your training partner's job even easier and enhance your training by giving you a faster turnover of techniques.

A suggestion for numbers and techniques to use are as follows:

- one = jab
- two = jab and cross
- three = jab, cross and lead hook
- four = jab, cross, lead hook and rear hook
- five = jab, cross, lead hook, rear hook and lead uppercut
- six = jab, cross, lead hook, rear hook, lead uppercut and rear uppercut

Your training partner can either call out isolated numbers such as one, two or three and so on, or they can group numbers together such as two and three, so you would do a jab and cross, then immediately perform another jab, cross and lead hook.

Work this drill for a set period of time and include adequate rest over a series of rounds (for example, 2min rounds with 1min rest and working to five rounds in total).

Training Drill 6

Shadow Sparring (With a Static Partner)

This drill can be used in several different ways. Initially, you will need a training partner to assist you and you can work together, taking rest periods while the other trains. The overall objective of this drill involves one person shadow sparring (without making contact) in front of their training partner in the usual way. Use your footwork, movement, attacks, counters, defences and evasions, but keep your training partner in view, either full view or just enough so that you can still see them peripherally.

The training partner holds a focus pad up high and at any given time they release the pad so that it drops to the floor. At that point, you perform a technique or combination of techniques before

Fig. 441   Static shadow-sparring drill.

the pad hits the ground. When it does, you continue shadow sparring while your training partner retrieves the pad and sets it up for round two.

The alternative with this drill is to nominate a technique and, as the pad is released, attempt to perform as many of those techniques as possible before the pad hits the floor (Fig. 441)

Training Drill 7

Partner Shadow Sparring

This training drill is not only going to improve your shadow-sparring ability, it will also help you to develop your explosive speed. You can either wear your protective sparring equipment for this one, or choose to go bare knuckle but with caution. My advice would be to glove up if your targeting and control are not yet fully developed.

You need two training partners for this drill – one to shadow spar with and the other to call out the instructions. Face your training partner in your fighting stance and begin shadow sparring. Don't actually make contact at this point, but

Fig. 442   Use your partner as a target.

Fig. 443   Continue to attack without contact.

Fig. 444   When the command is given you both try to land a clean shot.

instead use your partner as a living punch bag, focusing on attacking the areas left open. They should randomly change stance and guard in order to assist you with this.

Then, when the second training partner calls 'Now!', you both attack with a nominated technique to an open area on the other's head or body. The first one to land the attack scores a point. Then you remain stationary while your training partner starts shadow sparring and, again, when the second training partner shouts 'Now!', you both attack once more. Continue the drill for a set period of time, then swap places.

Add an element of competition by introducing a forfeit for the lowest scoring person, either by using an overall score or a score after each round (Figs 442 to 444).

Training Drill 8

Shadow-Freeze Sparring

This training drill works along similar lines to the previous one, but with a slight twist on the end. As before, face off with your partner and start shadow sparring (Figs 445 and 446). Use the open areas that your training partner creates as your target points, but do not actually make con-

tact, especially with bare knuckle. Use your footwork, attacks, kicks, punches, defences and evasions (even though your partner will not be attacking back, you still need to simulate the defences so that you get used to defending). Your training partner can move around and change their guard to add realism to the drills, but they can't attack back.

Then, when your second training partner shouts 'Freeze!', your first training partner freezes in their position while you attack an open gap with any explosive technique, aiming to land the shot (just be careful of head or face shots when doing this). Use the best technique that fits the gap based on your position at the time (Fig. 447). Continue, but switch roles (so you become the target and your partner shadows and attacks). Continue for a set amount of time, then swap round.

Variations on this drill are to have the second training partner call the name of the person they want to freeze, or you can number yourselves so that the caller shouts, for example, 'One, freeze!'. The other person then has to perform the attack before switching roles (so regardless of who attacks each time, the shadow sparring is still alternated).

Fig. 445   Shadow spar without contact.

Fig. 446   Continue to attack using your partner as a target.

Training Drill 9

Shadow Sparring With Blockers

Although we've left this one until last, this final drill is actually a good one to start off with if you're not used to shadow sparring, as it will help you get used to the movements that you make when you shadow. If you are used to shadow sparring, and you may well be by this stage, then add it in as a final drill to enhance your shadow sparring ability even further.

Face a training partner who is holding a pair of blockers. As they hold them out in front, use them to focus your attacks. You do not have to hit them every time (or at all if you prefer not to), but they are there and are designed in such a way that you can attack them from any angle without the need for your training partner to move them (unlike focus pads, the square shape and total padding of a blocker means that you can actually hit them at any angle, front, side or top, regardless of how they are being held).

Fig. 447   Your partner freezes and you attack a scoring zone.

Your partner can also attack you back with them, which in turn allows you to practise your defences and evasions as well as your counter-attacks (Figs 448 to 451). Work this for a set time based on your level of fitness. Use the table at the start of the book as a guide.

TOP LEFT: Fig. 448   Using the blockers as targets while shadowing.

TOP RIGHT: Fig. 449   Evade attacks.

BELOW LEFT: Fig. 450   Use the blockers to shadow with while kicking.

BELOW RIGHT: Fig. 451   Use the blockers to defend while shadowing.

13 Developing Pad Work

There is a saying in the martial-arts (and boxing) world that a pad feeder will either make or break the training drill. Amazingly, and not everyone realizes this, pad feeding (the term given when holding a pair of focus pads for someone to hit) is, in itself, a skill and the better you are at feeding pads, the better the workout your training partner gets. As with any skill, the more you do it, the better you become at it and so for that reason we're going to devote a whole chapter of this book to the skilled art of pad feeding.

Watch any top-level fighter train and you will clearly see that aside from natural talent and ability, a great deal of their training and fighting ability has come from the skills of their coaches and training partners. Watch how these people hold, move and work pads in order to get the best out of their fighter and you will start to understand how a great deal of the success of that fighter is in the hands of the people who set the training.

We are not all fortunate enough to be in a position to have a whole team of coaches there for the sole purpose of turning us into the best fighters we can possibly become. For most, we have to rely on people who also train with us (our training partners). Their (and your) understanding and ability of how to use a pair of focus pads, kick shield or any other training aid for that matter will make the difference between us becoming great fighters, or just run-of-the-mill martial artists – and there are a lot of run-of-the-mill martial artists.

So, although it would seem that we are going slightly off the beaten track with this chapter, having a good understanding of how to use the training aids you have around you will, in turn, not only help to make you a better training partner, but it will actually help to make you a better fighter. Ask any instructor and they will tell you

that their knowledge and understanding of their chosen art and in turn their ability within that art will have grown considerably from simply teaching and passing on their knowledge to their students. I know it did with me.

Having a better understanding of how to use a pair of focus pads, how to hold them, move them, set them up, attack with them and so on will certainly benefit all those who train with you, but at the same time it will also add another string to your bow and allow you to pass that knowledge on to your training partners, which will in turn raise your level. Just be aware that a good pad feeder will be just as worn out at the end of the drill as the person they are holding pads for ...

IMPORTANT – Ensure that you have warmed up and stretched correctly before moving on to the following training drills. Use the training guides at the start of the book to assist you.

Before we start with the training drills I want to teach you how to hold a pair of focus pads properly. This is important because there is a correct way to hold them and hundreds of incorrect ways. With the focus pads on, stand in a fighting stance in exactly the same way that you would if you were about to face off against an opponent. Hold your hands up in a guard position, placing your rear hand on your chin and your lead hand out in front of you (Fig. 452).

When you want your partner to stop attacking the pads, you bring them back into this position, or you bring them back and place them on your chest. When I hold pads for people, I like to bring them back to a guard position. This simple action helps me to condition myself to keep my guard up as well. Even though I'm not fighting, I believe that constant repetition helps to make

Fig. 452   How to hold a pair of focus pads.

things instant and natural, so for that reason I would rather condition myself to bring the pads back to a guard instead of to my chest, for when I really need to do it.

As you present a pad to be hit, hold out the same hand as the one your partner will be hitting with. For example, if we're both standing in a left lead (you need to mirror your partner with this as well), and I want my partner to use their right hand to punch with, I hold my right-hand pad out (Fig. 453). At this point, I will place the pad not in use on the chest. This clearly tells my training partner that this pad is not in use.

If you want your training partner to attack two pads, you hold two pads out in front (Fig. 454). Although they won't hit them both at the same time, this tells your partner that they are to send out two attacks (for example, a jab and a cross), so they know to explode with both before returning to their guard position.

A kick shield is held differently, as you would naturally expect, although the type of kick shield

Fig. 453   Hold out a right pad for a right punch.

Fig. 454   Hold out two pads for a double attack.

Fig. 455   How to hold a kick shield.

Fig. 456   Pull the kick shield into the body.

that you have determines how you hold it. The general idea is that you place your strongest arm through the horizontal straps and your weakest hand grabs the vertical handle (Fig. 455). You then stand side on and pull the kick shield into the body (Fig. 456).

The tendency with this is to hold the kick shield out in front of you and away from the body, but what then happens is that every time the shield is kicked, the power of the kick will drive the pad back into your body (with some considerable force). The pad absorbs the energy of each attack better if it is pulled in close as shown.

Training Drill 1

Single Pad Feeding
This training drill will help you to understand how to hold the focus pads for single-hand attacks. As previously mentioned, when pad feeding you generally hold the same hand out as the one you want your partner to strike with. For

example, to get your partner to use their lead jab (left hand) when in a left lead, you hold out your left pad (Fig. 457).

To get them to work their cross punch (right hand), you hold out your rear (right) pad (Fig. 458). If you want them to work a rear hooking punch, you hold out your rear pad, but you change the angle of it so that it now faces inward (Fig. 459). And if you want them to work their lead uppercut, you hold out your lead hand and again change the angle of it so that it faces the floor (Fig. 460).

The key to this is to make the pad positions as realistic as possible. For example, if your training partner was actually going to strike you on the nose, when feeding pads for this you need to position the pad so that it is level with your nose. If you study Fig. 457, you will see that the pad is held in line with the head and level with the nose. If you drew a straight line from the puncher's fist to the pad feeder's nose, you would see that they would connect.

Look at the hooking punch in Fig. 459. You

Fig. 457   Single pad feeding for a jab.

Fig. 458   Single pad feeding for a cross.

Fig. 459   Single pad feeding for a hook.

Fig. 460   Single pad feeding for an uppercut.

Fig. 461 Pad position for an axe kick.

Fig. 462 Pad position for a jumping kick.

will see that the pad is held in line with the head, as the attack would be aimed at the side of the head or side of the chin. There is no point or benefit to your partner holding the pad way out to the right, as this gives them a false target.

Finally, observe the pad position for the upper-cut in Fig. 460. As the target area is the chin, the pad is held out level with the pad feeder's chin and on the same centreline. There would be no point in holding it any higher or lower, as this would give the puncher a false target.

Other attacking angles to use with a pair of focus pads include the position for an axe kick, in which the kick needs to clear the lead shoulder and then attack the side of the face (Fig. 461) and the jumping front kick, in which the ball of the foot needs to strike the chin area (Fig. 462).

The first stage to feeding pads successfully is to make the distance and angles of attack as realistic as possible.

Training Drill 2

Double Pad Feeding

The double pad feed is probably the technique you will use the most, particularly when feeding pads to develop cardio, as it is the easiest way to double the workload of your training partner without the necessity to talk to them as you train. There are several ways to hold the pads for a double attack, for example straight on as shown in figs 463 and 464, which enables the puncher to

Fig. 463 Double pad feeding for a jab ...

Fig. 464 ... and a cross combo.

161

work techniques such as the jab and the cross (observe how the lead pad is held slightly ahead of the rear pad to encourage the puncher to move into the rear punch).

They can also be held side on so that both pads face in toward each other; this is normally used for hooking punches or backfist strikes. With this method, lower the lead pad once it has been hit to prevent it from getting in the way of the second attack. The pads can also both be held so that they face the floor; this is ideally used for uppercut attacks. Again, bring the lead pad slightly ahead of the rear pad to encourage your partner to work their body mechanics as they punch.

From here, you can start playing about with the pad positions, for example holding the lead pad out straight for a jab and the rear pad facing in for a hooking punch. Alternatively, hold the lead pad facing in for a lead hook and the rear pad facing straight for a cross punch.

In the same way as you did with the single pad drills, after each double attack bring the pads back to your guard position or back to the chest, whichever you prefer, and move around (as if you were both sparring), so that you also get a chance to work your footwork.

Try working double pads with a training partner for a set amount of time based on your partner's fitness levels, as it is your training partner who will be expending most of the energy.

Training Drill 3

Multiple Pad Feeding

Having an ability to feed pads so that your training partner can work multiple techniques is probably the most beneficial. For this to work, however, you need to be fast enough (and confident enough) to move the pads into position so that they are there to meet the punches and/or kicks as they are thrown. For this type of pad feeding, you will also need to talk to your partner so that they know exactly what you want them to do.

In order for this to work smoothly, the best time to talk to your partner is during the movement/footwork stage in-between their attacks. For example, with the pads held in your guard position or on your chest, whichever you prefer,

you give the command 'cross, uppercut, hook' and your partner then responds by sending a rear-hand cross punch to your rear pad, instantly followed by a lead-hand uppercut to your lead pad, followed again by a rear-hand hooking punch to the rear pad (Figs 465 to 467). If they follow the simple rule that each hand works alternately, then it is relatively easy to remember that left follows right and vice versa.

On the other hand, should you want to start with a hooking punch attack, the puncher needs to observe which pad you hold out first before they start their punch. This will tell them how the punches should flow. Finally, should you want them to attack with the same hand twice, you need to tell them this. A command of 'double lead hook' tells your partner that you are expecting them to throw two hooking punches off the lead hand. A quick look at how you are holding the pads before they start the first punch will tell them exactly how you expect them to do this.

Combinations of more than three punches work as long as you talk to your partner between attacks. I personally find it is better to give them

Fig. 465   Multiple pad feeding for a jab ...

Fig. 466   ... uppercut.

Fig. 467   ... and hook combination.

the whole string of attacks then let them punch, as opposed to calling out each punch one at a time. The puncher can then explode with their multiple attacks, as opposed to having to strike then wait for the next instruction.

Try working multiple attack combinations with your training partner for a set duration based on their level of fitness.

Training Drill 4

Defensive Training

The focus pads are used a great deal in developing the defences and being able to feed pads for this purpose is a skill in itself. When people first start attacking back with the pads, there seems to be a big concern about making contact, almost in the same way as there is when a student first starts sparring. It's probably down to human nature and that for the vast majority of us, actually attacking someone, even if there is a benefit in it, goes against everything we are taught in society.

Unfortunately, when you take this approach to defensive training you actually do your training partner no favours, as you lead them into a false sense of security because most people can defend against half-hearted attacks, with little to no effort. What then happens as that person becomes used to defending like this is that when they find themselves in a sparring (or street) situation where they receive a full-contact attack, they have no way of defending against it properly and usually come off worse.

When using the pads to develop the defences, you ideally need to make the attacks a real as possible without actually injuring your partner and, providing they defend that attack properly, the risk of causing any real injury is greatly reduced. In order to simulate a realistic attack, you need to start off slowly and build up the power. Begin by over-exaggerating the attack, striking with about 50 per cent force, so that your training partner can clearly see it coming and can defend against it. Then evaluate how effective their defence was before striking again. There is no point in sending

Fig. 468   Working a straight pad defence for a jab.

Fig. 469   Working a straight pad defence for a cross.

Fig. 470   Working a circular pad defence for a hooking punch attack.

Fig. 471   Working a rising pad defence against an uppercut attack.

a faster, harder attack if they failed to defend the previous one effectively. If you need to, stop the drill and go back to Chapter 9, 'Developing the Defences', before moving on any further. If their defence was effective enough, move around a little using your footwork and attack again.

Build up the speed and power of the attack as you feel your partner become more efficient with their defences. But remember, this training drill is not about you attacking your partner. As with all pad feeding, it's about you working with your partner to help them develop their defensive ability.

Start off by sending a single straight attack as shown in Figs 468 to 471, for a set period of time. Then by using the attacks outlined in Chapter 9 as a guide, isolate a different attacking method and work this in the same way.

A variation on this drill is to add in random, single attacks so that your partner does not know what is coming and really has to focus on the drill. Once they are proficient at defending random attacks, add in an attack back every time you feed the pads to get them into the habit of defending instead of just attacking all the time.

Training Drill 5

Countering the Attack

This drill is going to help you get used to attacking your training partner with a pair of focus pads and then positioning them back to receive counters. It combines all of the skill developed so far, as you will be attacking, talking to your partner and holding the pads for a multiple attack combination. In order for this to work smoothly, your pad-feeding ability needs to be at a level where you can feed the pads for multiple attacks with ease, you understand basic footwork and movement and you can think quickly on your feet so that the drills are kept fast-paced without you having to stop and think about the next combination.

Start out by telling your partner what's going to happen. The level of your partner here will determine exactly how much information you

Fig. 472   Send an attack using the pads.

Fig. 473   Position the pad for a counter-strike.

Fig. 474   A second counter-strike.

Fig. 475   A third counter-strike.

give them. For example, if they have little experience punching pads, you might give the command 'defend a jab and counter with a cross, lead hook, cross'. If they are quite experienced, you might simply say 'defend, cross, hook, cross' (Figs 472 to 475). The first instruction is simply to defend whatever you send at them, then counter straight back with a cross, hook and cross. If you want them to defend against several attacks, you can tell them what you are going to throw, or you can simply say 'defend, defend' plus whatever the counter is. Basically, as long as you are talking to your partner throughout, there is less chance of miscommunication and the drill runs a lot more smoothly.

Training Drill 6

Follow Me Drills

This type of pad-feeding drill removes the necessity for you to talk to your partner, which means that the drills can run much more quickly as

there is less of a pause in-between. This time, hold out the pads for your training partner to hit, then simply return the same attacks. For example, hold the two pads out in front to simulate a jab, cross combination from your partner, and as soon as the jab, cross has landed, immediately return a jab and a cross toward your partner for them to defend (Figs 476 to 477).

Base the speed of your attacks on your partner's training ability so that they have a chance of defending against them. As mentioned previously, this drill is about feeding the pads well so that your partner has an opportunity to practise their punching and defending. It is not about you trying to smash your partner in the face as hard as you can. If their training level is high, you can work more of the multiple pad-feeding drills such as those in training drill 3. Your partner then knows what defences they will need to perform, based on what they had to throw. This means that you will have to start talking to your partner in order for the drill to work.

Fig. 476   Position the pads for a jab ...

Fig. 477   ... and a cross.

Fig. 478   Return a jab ...

Fig. 479   ... and a cross.

Training Drill 7

Reaction Pad Drills

This pad-feeding drill is a spin on the traditional pad-feeding methods and adds something different to the training. It also helps to break the monotony of simply holding pads out in front for your training partner to strike. The objective of this pad drill is to develop the peripheral vision of your training partner, a valuable skill required for sparring.

Stand facing your training partner in your fighting stance wearing one pad on your lead hand and placing the other hand (without the pad) on your chest. Your partner then stands in their fighting stance in the usual way. With your training partner primed and ready to fire out a punch, simply raise a finger as a signal for them to attack the pad (Fig. 480). To add a level of realism to the drill, move around after each punch so as to develop the footwork.

Fig. 480   Reaction pad drills.

Fig. 481   Reaction kick shield drills.

Ensure your training partner is not focusing on your finger movement and instead focuses on the chest area as a whole. As described in Chapter 11, 'Developing Sparring', you need to ensure you focus on the chest area of your training/sparring partner so that you see everything. Remember, if you focus on the kick, you won't see the punch.

Train this drill for a set period of time and vary the punches used.

Training Drill 8

Reaction Kick Shield Drills

This drill works in the same way as the previous one, except that a kick shield is now used instead of a focus pad and kicks are worked instead of punches. This time, the signal for your training partner to kick is a movement of the lead foot. If you incorporate footwork into this drill as suggested in the previous one, I would recommend you stop, set yourself up and then raise the lead foot off the floor, otherwise your training partner won't actually be able to tell the difference between a signal and a simple movement.

Try to make the signal as subtle as possible. For example, a raise of the toes as opposed to raising the whole foot off the floor is all that's required for your partner to attack (Fig. 481). Again, try to instil the importance of them focusing on you as opposed to your foot, as this would be a really bad habit to get in to.

Training Drill 9

Kick Shield Drills

We have focused a great deal on the focus pads and the reason for this is because out of all the training aids, these are probably the most versatile as they can be used for developing the full range of kicks, punches, elbows and knee strikes, as well as being used for attacking back with more realism and ease of use than most other training aids can. However, as a kicking training aid, you can't actually beat the kick shield, especially for developing power in the kicks. Admittedly, the Thai pad serves an excellent purpose when developing kicks and punches together, but for isolating kicking techniques I personally find the kick shield to be the best when training with a partner (try receiving a full-contact spinning back kick on a pair of Thai pads and see what happens).

In this drill you simply move around using your footwork while holding the kick shield in various positions so that your partner can isolate their kicking techniques. For this drill to run smoothly, you will need to talk to your training partner and tell them how many and what types of kicks you are expecting with each movement. The best way to do this is to give them the instruction as you are moving around in-between kicks, then stop and let them kick before continuing (Figs 482 and 483).

Work this training drill for a set time period and a set number of rounds at your discretion.

Fig. 482   Hold the kick shield for a side kick.

Fig. 483   Hold the kick shield for a round kick.

Training Drill 10

Circle Reaction

By now, you should be familiar with how to use a kick shield and a pair of focus pads (or Thai pads) in order to get the best out of your training partner and add variety to your drills. We are therefore going to spend the next few drills looking at ways in which you can use the same training aids to help you develop training drills for multiple partners. This way, you give your training partners a different kind of training experience and add an element of competition to your drills.

Hold a kick shield and stand in the middle of a group of up to four other participants. Ensure your training partners distribute themselves evenly around you as shown in Fig. 484. Number each person starting from one (for example, one, two, three and four). Then nominate a kick or combination of kicks and when you call out a number, the person with the corresponding number runs to the appropriate position and strikes the kick shield (Fig. 485). As the pad holder, you can choose to remain stationary throughout the drill, or you can randomly change direction so that each person has an equal chance of hitting the kick shield.

Variations to this drill involve each kicker performing a set number of kicks (for example, ten round kicks), while the other members of the circle perform a set number of exercises (for example, five push-ups). The kicker needs to try to finish before those doing the exercises and gets a penalty point if not. At the end of all the rounds,

Fig. 484   Position yourself in the middle of a circle.

Fig. 485   As you call the number, that kicker attacks.

Fig. 486   Attack the corresponding pad when the number is called.

Fig. 487   Turn to attack another number.

the person with the most penalty points gets a forfeit.

Alternatively after each kick or combination of kicks, the person returns to their spot and performs a nominated exercise (for example, five sit-ups). Vary the number and intensity of the exercises and kicks to match the level of the people in your team. Work each drill for a set time based on the fitness levels of your partners. To keep the drills high in energy and fast-paced, I would suggest no longer than 1min per pad holder.

Training Drill 11

Reaction Focus Pad Drills 1

This training drill works in the same way as the previous one, except you now use focus pads instead of a kick shield and you focus on punches

instead of kicks. The focus pads instead of the kick shield can be used for the previous drill if you prefer, as both types of training aid will give you a different training experience.

Training Drill 12

Reaction Focus Pad Drills 2

This time, the pad feeders remain on the outside of the circle and the puncher stands in the middle. Each pad feeder is now given a number as before and one of the pad feeders becomes the controller. The controller controls the action by calling out one number at a time. As they do, the puncher has to turn to face the person with the corresponding number and strike the pad with a nominated technique (Fig. 486). As soon as they have done this, the controller calls out the next number.

As the controller of the drill, ensure you keep the person in the middle moving as fast as possible by keeping the number-calling fast enough so that they are not standing still and having to wait. At the same time, do not call the numbers out so quickly that they are unable to keep up with your pace.

A variation on this drill is simply to strike the pad as fast as possible by utilizing your footwork as effectively as you can. For example, instead of staying in a left lead in order to strike the pad each time, simply turn to the next pad as expediently as possible and strike the pad with whichever lead happens to be in front at the time (Fig. 487).

Training Drill 13

Add in Defences
This drill simply involves adding in an attack from the pad feeder either before or after each attack from the puncher, so that the puncher can also work their defences. For example, as the number is called, the puncher turns to face that pad, then performs the appropriate technique (such as a jab). Immediately after they strike the pad, the pad feeder attacks back. This can either be a nominated attack, or it can mirror the attack that the puncher uses. The rest of the drill then continues as in training drill 12.

Option two is to attack the puncher as they turn, thereby ensuring the puncher maintains a good solid guard throughout the whole of the drill. A common mistake with the puncher is to let the guard hang a little low. This naturally brings with it a risk of being hit and is therefore an ideal drill to ensure that this area is also worked thoroughly.

Option three simply involves adding both defences together, one before the attack and one after.

Training Drill 14

Attack the Back
The alternative to training drill 12 is to remove the number-calling and this time initiate the turn by simply hitting the back of the puncher with the focus pad. As they feel the attack land, they turn to face the pad feeder that they think attacked and attack that pad with a nominated technique or combination. This drill brings together all of the elements of the last two drills, but with a physical turn indicator rather than an auditory one.

There still needs to be a controller to maintain order throughout the training drill. The only difference now is that they no longer call out the number of the pad feeder who needs to attack, but instead simply nod or gesture toward them. The puncher in the middle probably won't pick up on this due to the intensity of the drill, therefore it would appear that the attacks are happening randomly.

Defences and counters can be added in as before. Just ensure that the signal for the puncher to attack (the slap on the back) is done purely to instigate a reaction and not with any unnecessary power, which could increase the possibility of injury.

Training Drill 15

Pad Circle
This time, the pad feeders circle the person in the middle and everyone holds out a focus pad placed on the same hand. The person in the middle then has to strike each pad with a round kick without placing their foot down or dropping their knee (Figs 488 to 490). This drill is a great one for developing pad-feeding skills, due to the fact that all the pad feeders need to work together as a team.

Once the person in the middle has hit every pad with the nominated technique for the agreed number of rounds (for example, hit every pad with a round kick five times before stopping), they then switch places with one of the pad feeders. Continue until everyone has gone, then change the kick and the pad position.

A variation to this drill is to hold the pads at varying heights so that the kicker has to kick to the head, body or leg each time. Alternatively, you can instruct the pad feeders to hold the pads at different angles so that the kicker has to work different kicks based on how the pads are held. For example, a front-on pad position might mean a front kick or possibly a side kick, whereas a side-on pad position might mean a round kick or possibly a hooking kick, depending on how it is held.

Training Drill 16

The Variations

This final drill will help you to understand the additional elements that you could add in to your pad-feeding drills. This way, once you get familiar with pad feeding and your confidence and skill levels grow, you need only have a theme in mind when you start feeding the pads to find that you will be able to put together specific training drills on the spot with relative ease.

Areas in which to develop pad feeding for the kick:

- power
- footwork – start 'out of range' and use footwork to close the gap
- speed – strike as fast as possible but without adding power
- jump – develop the kick as a jumping version of the static one

Fig. 488 Kick the first pad.

Fig. 489   Keep the knee high.

Fig. 490   Strike the next pad.

- spin – develop the kick as a spinning version of the static one
- jump and spin – develop the kick as a jumping spinning version of the static one.

Areas in which to develop pad feeding for the punch:

- lead-hand attacks only
- rear-hand attacks only

- double attacks only, for example both attacks off the same hand
- alternate attacks only, for example both attacks off each hand
- body and head – attacks that target the body and head, for example a hook to the body and a hook to the head
- head and body – attacks that target the head and body, for example a hook to the head and a hook to the body.

14 Developing the Mind

Although this chapter has come at the end of the book (and there is a reason for this), I personally believe it to be the most important. Too many times I have witnessed students with real potential fail to make a name for themselves in the martial-arts world because of their lack of mental belief. It doesn't matter who you are, what talents you have, how hard you work or what natural talent you have been blessed with, if your mind does not believe that you are worth the prize you are striving for, you will never achieve it.

The mind is an incredibly powerful tool and many books have been written on the subject. When you break it down and analyse it, the mind coupled with your belief system (that is, do you believe you are good enough or deserve what it is you are after) can be traced back to your successes and failures in every part of your life. How many goals have you had over the course of your life that you have failed to achieve? If the answer to the question is that you have achieved everything you set out to achieve, then well done, your belief system is clearly first rate so you can skip this chapter. If, like the rest of us, however, you are still smoking, still in that mundane job, still intend to write that book, still buy your dream car, still to win that world title, then read on.

Although I'm no qualified mind-development expert (is there such a thing?), I understand enough about the power of the mind from my research and experience to be able to pass on my knowledge and understanding in this chapter. Just be aware that this chapter will look simply to touch on what the mind is capable of in order to give you a basic understanding of how to achieve your goals and ambitions. For further study, I would advise you to buy a book on the subject and do your own research, or, if time allows, start a sports psychology course or similar.

The problem we have in today's society is that life travels at 100mph and as a consequence we all want instant results. Some of us want instant results without actually being prepared to put in the effort – just look at the National Lottery as the greatest example of this. Martial-arts training is no different. In the past it would take many years to achieve the grade of black belt and each black-belt student would have gone through a rigorous training programme in order to achieve this level, a training programme that would have focused as much on the mental side of the art as the physical. In today's society, however, you can join a fast-track programme and achieve a black belt in around twelve months if you choose the right school (or the wrong school as the case would be). In reality, this new generation of black-belt students will fail to have the physical development or experience needed to be able to back up their grade, let alone have the mental development required for someone at this level.

The reason this chapter has come at the end of the book is because the physical side of your training is the easiest part to develop, so it is this side of your development that we can begin our training with. Developing the mental aspect is a lot harder to do as it's not tangible, so for that reason the results are harder to measure. With the physical aspect, you can clearly see and measure the results through an improvement in your fitness, flexibility, speed and power, whereas the mental aspect is a lot slower to develop.

When I first started training, I would watch, in total admiration, as the high-grade students trained and sparred and I would think to myself how incredible it would be to be that good, always secretly thinking that it was 'everybody else' who became good and not me. As I got more into my art, however, I decided to start training more and that resulted in my level improving far more quickly. Soon my level surpassed that of my training partners, who were still only training the bare minimum and I consequently moved up to the senior levels with relative ease, while my original training partners started quitting. Thereafter I increased my training once again until those that I once admired were coming to me for help and inspiration. Not long after this I achieved my first black belt and it was then that I realized the true potential of the mind – the harder I worked, the better I became and the better I became, the more I started to believe. The more I started to believe, the harder I worked …

Since that day I have used the lessons I learnt when I was younger to achieve a great deal with my life and this book is proof of that. Having a strong belief system, coupled with a 'never give up' attitude, will carry you through and help you to achieve anything you want in life. The problem with today's society is that people quit too easily and are not prepared to put in the hard work required to achieve their goals. I once read somewhere that it takes ten years to become an overnight success. Keep that in mind and appreciate that if you have tried something a couple of times and had no success, then you clearly have not tried hard enough. Read the biographies of successful people to understand exactly what is involved in getting to the top. Although this chapter might not make you a millionaire or a rock star, it will certainly help you believe in yourself enough to bring your training up to the next level and if you use this as a starting point, you never actually know where that next step might take you …

IMPORTANT – Ensure that you have warmed up and stretched correctly before moving on to the following training drills. Use the training guides at the start of the book to assist you.

Will Drills

The first thing we're going to do is condition the mind to not accept defeat and we do this in the form of 'will drills'. The challenge that every mar-

Quitting vs Self-Belief

Quitting does not necessarily mean giving up. You can quit by simply taking the easier option. As most of your training in the martial arts involves you having to push yourself, it actually takes a certain kind of person with the correct attitude and mindset, who can push themselves hard all of the time. For a lot of students, the easy way is the preferred way. Remember the phrase, 'how you train is how you fight'.

Quitting does not just refer to physical training. If a fighter does not believe in their ability, particularly in the run-up to a competitive fight as a great example, they can lose before they have even stepped onto the mats (or cage or boxing ring). As a result, if you don't believe in yourself, you will fail.

tial-arts student has regarding the mind is the problem with giving up or accepting defeat. This refers to developing elements such as flexibility (for example, stretching to develop flexibility can be an uncomfortable experience, so people stop doing it), right through to developing their overall training (for example, they stop training and quit altogether). Even simple training drills that fatigue the body can result in students accepting the easier option of taking it slightly easier instead of pushing themselves through that barrier when the going gets tough. For that reason, will drills are a great training aid for developing that 'never give up' attitude and pushing through when you might otherwise have taken it easy or just quit.

The following drills are designed to push you hard. You will probably train harder now than in all the other chapters of the book. The drills get tougher as you get further into them and it is at this point that you could be tempted to slow down or take a rest. My advice is not to, no matter how hard it gets. Push through until the end of the drill and when it starts to hurt, keep telling yourself that you are not going to quit.

Will Drill 1

Accumulating Kicks

This first drill is a good one to start with simply because it is relatively easy to grasp and easy enough to perform. However, don't be fooled by its simplicity. Sometimes the simplest drills are often the most demanding, as you will no doubt soon discover.

The drill works as follows. Using either a punch bag as your target, or a training partner holding a kick shield, you are going to strike the pad with one of the three basic kicks (round kick, side kick or front kick) as hard as you can. Once you have done one kick, you then perform two with no rest. Repeat the drill for three kicks and so on until you reach ten (start with one kick, then do two kicks, then do three kicks, then four and so on). In-between each kick, bounce the foot off the floor so that you not only kick as hard as you can, but you also perform each kick as fast as possible. Figs 491 to 493 show this drill in action.

Variations to this drill involve repeating the drill using the other leg without resting as soon as you have finished the first set, or working back down to one kick from ten (you go from ten kicks, down to nine, then eight, then seven and so on). This drill is very tough and a great one to start the will drills training with as you will want to quit or take a rest before you finish the whole drill. My advice is to not quit, regardless of how tough it gets, because if you do, you condition the mind to accept defeat.

Fig. 491   Kick the pad.

Fig. 492   Bounce the foot off the floor.

Fig. 493   Kick the pad again.

Fig. 494   Strike the pad with a jab ...

Fig. 495   ... then a cross.

Fig. 496   ... then a hook.

Fig. 497   ... and an uppercut.

Will Drill 2

Pyramid Punches

This drill gives the legs a little rest by solely utilizing the punches and therefore the upper body. Again, the drill can be performed on a punch bag if a training partner is not available. Alternatively, a training partner can hold a pair of focus pads for you. Sometimes it's good to train with a partner, as they can motivate and encourage you throughout the drills and prevent you from quitting or taking the easy option.

Start off by striking your target with a jab using speed and power. Then immediately perform a jab and a cross, followed by a jab, cross and lead hook and finally a jab, cross, hook and rear uppercut. You then work back down to the jab (for example, jab, cross, hook, then jab, cross, then jab), before starting again (Figs 494 to 497). Continue with the drill for a set period of time based on your fitness levels.

Will Drill 3

Squat Kicks

This drill will work the lower body once again. However, due to the constant workload placed on the legs, this one is very tough (if done properly, of course). The objective is to perform a deep squat, followed by a power front kick to a kick shield or punch bag, alternating between legs after each squat (for example, squat and then kick with the left leg, then squat and kick with the right leg).

Work this drill for a set period of time based on your levels of fitness and, as with the previous drills, do not give up, regardless of how tough it gets (Figs 498 and 499).

Fig. 498   Perform a squat.

Time Limits

When a drill involves performing to a time limit, it is easy to get caught up in the habit of 'pacing' yourself in order to last the distance, whereas a drill with no time limit, in which you continue until you finish, tends to make you push yourself a little harder. For example, if an instructor suggests a student performs push-ups for 1min, there's a good chance that the student will perform around twenty-five slow-paced push-ups. If that same student was instructed to perform twenty-five push-ups, however, they would most likely get them done in around 30sec. Try it on a training partner and see for yourself. This is a great example of how the mind works.

Fig. 499   Strike the pad with a front kick.

Will Drill 4

Jab, Cross, Side Step

This drill will give you an all-round workout due to the constant punching and leg movement. With this one, you strike one focus pad using a jab, cross, then side-step to bring yourself in line with the second pad and perform a jab, cross again (Figs 500 to 502). This drill requires a training partner holding a pair of focus pads some distance apart as shown in the photos. Alternatively, you can position two punch bags slightly apart (free-standing ones would be easier for this). Either way, make sure there is a large enough distance between them so that you have to perform a definite side step, otherwise the temptation is just to slight-step, or not move at all once you start to tire.

Work this drill for a set period of time based on your fitness levels.

Fig. 500   Strike the pad with a jab ...

Fig. 501   ... and a cross.

Fig. 502   Step to the side and repeat the jab, cross.

Will Drill 5

15:10

This drill is unique because you actually perform it in two parts. The first part involves you performing a kicking or punching technique for 15sec, followed by an exercise for 10sec. Perform the whole routine for a total of five times (Figs 503 and 504). The variations of techniques and exercises are limitless, but to get you started here are some suggestions:

- front kick and squats
- jab, cross and push-ups
- round kick and burpees
- lead and rear hooking punch and sit-ups
- side kick and star jumps.

Will Drill 6

The Ultimate Will Drill

This final drill is probably the toughest of all, as it involves using kicks and punches, performing core-conditioning exercises and picking yourself up off the floor constantly. You need to perform this drill for a set period of time based on your fitness levels as always. However, just be aware that over a period of 1min, you may only get to perform the whole drill a couple of times. Therefore, my suggestion for this one is to add an extra minute onto your normal training time period, using the table 'Training Times/Repetitions' at the start of the book as your guide.

The drill works as follows: start in a push-up position and perform one push-up (Fig. 505).

Fig. 503 Perform round kicks for 15sec.

Fig. 504 Perform squats for 10sec.

Jump through into a seated position (Fig. 506) and perform two round kicks (Fig. 507). Jump up into an upright position and perform a jab, cross, hook and uppercut on the pads (Fig. 508). Turn your back on the pads and step forward (Fig. 509) and perform a break fall (Fig. 510). Spin back around into your original push-up position and start the routine again (Fig. 511).

Desire

'Whatever the mind of man can conceive and believe, it can achieve.'

W. Clement Stone

This quote, although claimed by a few different people, actually sums up the potential power of the human mind. However, having an idea and believing in that idea alone is not enough and it is here that this concept falls flat and opens the floodgates for all the sceptics and non-believers. Firstly the idea, wish, goal, desire (call it what

Fig. 505   Start off in a push-up position.

Fig. 506   Jump into a seated position.

Fig. 507   Perform a double round kick.

Fig. 508   Jump back up to standing and perform a jab, cross, hook and uppercut.

Fig. 509   Turn around.

Fig. 510   Perform a break fall.

Fig. 511   Spin around into a push-up position and start again.

you like) needs to be realistic and actually achievable. For example, it is highly unlikely that a sixty-year-old kickboxer is going to win a full-contact world kickboxing title regardless of how much belief they have in their abilities. Not only that, but it also needs to be something that you can actually control or influence. World peace is a wonderful idea shared by millions of people, but until the whole world gets on board with this, it is probably not going to happen.

One of the reasons people fail to achieve their goals and dreams is because they set them too high. Don't focus on winning a world title before you have at least come in the top three at a local competition. Once you have that realistic goal or desire, you have to breathe life into it. Most desires fail to materialize, because, as with everything in life, they require an element of work on the part of the person involved. The larger the desire, the more work required to make it a reality.

Once you have that desire, you need to set a plan in motion for achieving it. Let's say, for example, that you want to buy a new car. Firstly, you need to know how much that new car is going to cost you before you sign the paperwork. Let's say it is going to cost you £500 per month and you are currently earning your living as a martial-arts instructor (let's keep it martial-arts related). You therefore need to determine a plan that will generate the extra £500 you need to keep up the payments. If you charge £30 per month for training fees, you will need an extra seventeen students signed up at your school before you can put your order in.

The first part is nice and simple. Now comes the hard part. How are you going to get those seventeen new students through the doors? This is where your marketing skills come into play (or your ability to pay for someone else's marketing skills, and don't forget to add this to your costings as well). Alternatively, you could put everyone's prices up, but you may lose a few students as a result of this move. It is at this point, once you realize how much work is involved in generating seventeen new members above and beyond your normal intake (and allowing for natural losses and cancellations), that you might decide to stick with the car you already have.

This is how the human mind works. It is easier to continue as you are and not have to put in that extra bit of work, than to step up to the mark and do more in order to achieve more. At least this way you still get to watch your favourite television programme each night while drinking your glass of wine and eating your takeaway meal, instead of having to go out and put leaflets through doors.

If you want to win a world title, write a book, break into martial-arts movies or anything else that you set for yourself, you need an action plan set in place in the same way as you would need a business plan if you wanted to start your own business. It's no different. Then, once you have that action plan in place, you need to follow it through with belief. You also need to add some contingency plans in there when things don't go the way you had planned, and it will happen. Life has a funny way of throwing a spanner in the works, almost to test how badly you really want something before awarding you the prize. It is here that most people would give up, saying 'Oh well, I tried but it wasn't meant to be ...' The achievers, however, always find a way.

Visualization

'Visualization is daydreaming with a purpose.'
Bo Bennett

Visualization is not a new concept and has been used by doctors and sportspeople for many years. Chuck Norris, during his competitive days, would use visualization before a fight and said that his ability to rehearse a fight over and over again in his mind actually helped him to secure many of his victories.

I remember using visualization myself when I first read about it. In my early tournament fighting days an event organizer opened a tournament called 'The Six Foot Series', in which the first-place trophy was 6ft tall. Second and third places were cheap-looking plastic medals, so I (along with everyone else) was desperate to win first place. The only problem was that I had never had a first place before and this event attracted the very best fighters from all over the country due to the prize on offer.

For a few weeks prior to the event I would visualize myself winning first place. I visualized the fights I would have, the moves I would use, the referee awarding me the win and ultimately being awarded the first-place trophy. I actually got so into visualizing that I started being able to feel the cold metal of the trophy in my hands as I lifted it up. It was all so realistic that I felt certain I would win.

The day of the tournament inevitably arrived, so I, along with my teammates, boarded the coach to the venue. After a few hours of waiting around while the other weight divisions fought, my category was eventually called, so I took my place alongside the rest of my opponents by the mats. I don't remember much about my fights on that day as it was many years ago, but I do know I lost in the early rounds and so that was that,

visualization clearly hadn't worked and was obviously a total waste of time.

Once the point-fighting categories had all finished, the event organizer announced over the tannoy that the registration for the light continuous categories was now starting and could any fighters taking part please come and register. As far as I was concerned, I had only ever been a point fighter and so had not planned to enter the light continuous section. However, something that day made me put my name down and I decided I was going to fight.

Amazingly, to this day I remember most of my fights. I managed to beat (with relative ease) all of my opponents to make it through to the final and take home the first-place trophy, the only trophy that I still have on display, kept in my home office where I'm writing this from right now (Fig. 512). Some might argue that visualization had nothing to do with it and that I just got lucky and they

Fig. 512   My 6ft trophy.

might be right, but one thing I do know is that if it was all just luck and visualization is a load of old nonsense, then I have been a very lucky person throughout my whole life, as I have used the same techniques as I did on that day many times since and all with the same end result.

The Subconscious Mind

While I was studying visualization, I came upon a great book called *Super Mind Training for Martial Arts*, by Dr Dan Lee. In it, he talks of a refrigerator test designed to help you develop your visualization skills. The test involves sitting quietly somewhere, closing your eyes and trying to picture your refrigerator as clearly as you can. It is fairly safe to say that the refrigerator is one household item that you would possibly use every day and yet, despite this fact, it is actually one that we don't consciously take much notice of. Subconsciously, however, we take everything in and by trying to engage with your subconscious mind during this test you are going to try to build a clear picture of your refrigerator in your mind's eye.

Picture the colour of it. Does it have an ice maker built in? Which side is the handle on? What material is the handle made out of? Listen to the noise it makes. Can you hear the gentle hum of the motor? It might be that you have to go and actually look at your refrigerator in order to do this and, if so, that's fine. Once you can clearly picture it in your mind, move to the next stage of the test and open the door.

As you open the door, how does the handle feel? Is it cold? What do you see inside? How many shelves does it have? What food do you have stored on each shelf? Does it have any drawers or compartments? What colour are they? Can you feel the cold air on your skin?

Your ability to recall all the small details about your refrigerator will help enormously when you start visualizing events and situations that you have not actually been in. Visualizing every minute detail such as smells, noises and sensations will make all the difference in being able to convince the mind that it is actually there. Geoff Thompson, in his book *Fear, the Friend of*

Exceptional People, talks about using visualization helping you to conquer your fears. He describes the brain finding it very difficult to tell the difference between what is real and what you have imagined and, as such, when you come to perform the goal you have been visualizing, the brain will ensure the body acts in the way it needs to in order to achieve this, as it believes you have actually performed the objective many times before.

A final word on this subject is to ensure that you use as many of the senses as you can when visualizing. Psychologists say that by using at least three of your five senses you will enhance your visualization practice. For that reason, do not just see the event play out in front of you – hear all the noises you would expect to hear, feel the sensations on your skin, smell the smells that you would expect to come across in that environment and, if necessary (if you take a drink of water during a rest period, for example), taste the things that you would expect to taste. Make the experience as real as possible so that there's no way your mind can think it is anything other than real.

Self-Hypnosis and Auto-Suggestion

Self-hypnosis and auto-suggestion are relatively similar. They are ways of reprogramming your belief system (the part of you that believes you can or can't do something) by sending a belief statement directly to your subconscious mind. The subconscious mind has been the subject of many books and studies and for further reading on the subject it would be worth visiting your local library or looking on the Internet. However, for now I'll offer a brief explanation of how the mind works.

Your conscious mind controls all of your thoughts, feelings and emotions and unfortunately these can be both positive and negative. It is said that 70 per cent of our daily thoughts are negative, so already we're off to a bad start. Our subconscious mind controls our belief system and it is this unconscious belief system that makes us act in the way we do. The thoughts, feelings and emotions that we allow to enter our conscious mind influence the subconscious mind and when enough of the same thoughts, feelings and emotions are absorbed, the subconscious mind acts on them. We have all heard the saying 'If you believe you're beaten, then you are' (and if you haven't heard it before, then you just have). This is where it comes from. If you keep telling yourself that you can't do something, or that you don't want to do something, your subconscious mind will eventually start to believe it and instruct your conscious mind to inform your body that you will fail. Fortunately for us, the same process works in reverse.

It takes approximately twenty-one days for a suggestion to be acted on by the subconscious mind and this is where self-hypnosis or auto-sug-gestion come in. Unfortunately, hypnosis has been given a bad name in recent years by the many stage magicians who hypnotize people into uncontrollably dancing around the stage like chickens, much to the amusement of everyone looking on. Firstly, this is a different kind of hyp-nosis; secondly, only certain types of people can actually be hypnotized in this way; and thirdly, you can't hypnotize someone to do something that they actually don't want to do or they believe (the belief system again) is morally or socially wrong, contrary to what you think you see them doing involuntarily.

Self-hypnosis, on the other hand, simply in-volves getting yourself into a relaxed state and repeating a suggestion to yourself, over and over again until the subconscious mind begins to be-lieve it, absorb it and therefore act upon it. Before we proceed any further, however, let's just clear a few things up regarding self-hypnosis. It's not magic. It will not allow you to perform the impos-sible. If you decide to use this method in order to help you win the Lottery, it won't work. You will find that a great deal of the 'get rich quick' or self-development books available on the market will use self-hypnosis or auto-suggestion as a way of changing your belief system so that you start to believe you are worth a million pounds (appar-ently, deep down a lot of us don't believe we are worth a million pounds, which is why we are not all millionaires, as wishing for something is totally different to actually believing it).

What self-hypnosis will do for you, over time, is change your belief system regarding the particu-lar thing that you are looking to achieve. Start off with something small and build up to the bigger goals. For example, if losing weight is something you are looking to do, start off by suggesting you lose a few pounds as opposed to a few stone. The few pounds are more achievable and therefore a great starting block to losing a few stone. Think of your martial-arts training like this. You would not try to learn a jumping, spinning hook kick before you could actually do a hook kick. You would never achieve it, get frustrated trying and eventually quit. Self-hypnosis and auto-sugges-tion are no different.

So, to begin with, you need to write down your belief statement. Keep it short and to the point so that it is easier to remember. Then you need to get into a relaxed state. The times when you are most relaxed are just before going to sleep and just before fully waking up, so these are the best times to perform this exercise. With your belief statement committed to memory, get yourself into your usual sleep position and relax. It will help if you take three deep breaths and actually say 'relax' to yourself with each breath. Then repeat the statement to yourself ten times. Each time you repeat the statement, visualize the event happening. As you visualize the event, inject it with feeling and emotion. This is important because the subconscious mind will only act on a suggestion that is emotionalized. Use the tech-niques you learnt in the last section on visualiza-tion to help you with this. Do the same thing again in the morning just before fully waking, then read the actual written statement to yourself before getting out of bed.

Do not miss a session or change the wording of your statement, otherwise you will have to start again from day one. Although it takes a minimum of twenty-one days for the subconscious mind to absorb something new, continue past this time for as long as you need to until you have achieved your goal. Also, do not be misled by the word 'hypnosis'. People believe that they should be in a trance-like state in order to be in a hypnotic state. This is actually a myth. Most of the time when someone is in an hypnotic state, they are still in full control of their actions. Instead, think of the correct state as simply a relaxed one. It is quite possible that you may be so relaxed that you actually fall asleep before reaching your tenth suggestion. This is actually fine, as you are most relaxed just before you fall asleep, therefore this is the perfect condition for your subconscious mind to be most receptive.

Once you become efficient at performing this, you can try putting yourself into a relaxed state during the day and repeating the exercise in order to super-charge its effectiveness. If you have a spare five minutes, find somewhere quiet, sit down, close your eyes, relax and then repeat your belief statement to yourself ten times with feeling and emotion in the usual way. Thereafter, if you are on the train or the bus, or even walking down the road, you can repeat your belief statement to yourself over and over again, picturing it coming true and feeling all the emotions that you will experience when you achieve it.

Anchors and Triggers

It is said that the Ninja would practise self-hypnosis in order to develop and hone their skills. In doing so, they would anchor some kind of a trigger to their auto-suggestion so that by simply activating the trigger they would instantly achieve the correct state of mind for that skill. An anchor could be something simple, such as touching a particular point on the body at the same time as performing the auto-suggestion. The trigger would then involve simply touching the anchor point to bring about the state of mind required to perform that particular task efficiently.

Imagine laughing so hard that it hurt. We've all been there and can all think back to such a time. Remember the endorphin release that laughing so hard brought about. Remember how great it felt and all the good feelings that were released with each moment. Then imagine that each time you laughed a friend patted you on the back. That pat on the back locks in (or anchors) a trigger. Years later, way after the event has passed, someone pats you on the back in the same way. They will instantly activate the trigger that will put you back into the same frame of mind as you were in all those years ago.

Smells (the scent that an old partner used to wear), songs (that you used to listen to when you were a child), pictures, places, voices, accents, faces are just a few of the many triggers that bring back all the memories, emotions and states of mind that we experienced when they were first anchored in many years ago.

Understanding this is a very powerful tool and can be used to help you achieve certain states of mind with instant effect. Imagine being in a stressful situation, just about to step onto the mats in a competition, perform at a demonstration, take a grading or even partake in something outside of your martial-arts world. Then imagine being able to relax yourself, heighten your awareness, release endorphins or generate a massive boost of energy, simply by activating a trigger. It is a reality and is the process of using anchors and triggers in this way. Be aware, though, that you can also lock in negative emotions and feelings in the same way.

Goal-Setting

Goal-setting works in conjunction with self-hypnosis and auto-suggestion and is a great way to end both this chapter and the book, as it is the final tool that you can use in order to help you develop the correct mindset with which to achieve everything you are striving for in your training (or your life, for that matter). The most important thing with having goals is to write them down. By committing yourself to writing them down, you begin the very first stage of your total commitment to achieving the goal. Think of it as the first step on your next journey, as that's what each goal is. By writing down what you want to achieve, you actually commit to it. Write down exactly what it is that you want to achieve and add in a realistic time frame by which to achieve it. This is important, otherwise there's no actual commitment to it. It is like organizing a wedding without actually setting a date. How could you possibly get everything ready in time?

Once you have written down your goal, you then need to put together an action plan detailing how you will achieve it. Again this is important, otherwise there will be no structure to it and you could actually end up anywhere. Imagine deciding one morning that you are going to take a drive to Stornoway in the Outer Hebrides, then just jumping in your car and driving off without doing any planning. You would probably never actually get there, more than likely get lost on the way and almost certainly give up and head back home.

Then imagine spending some time planning the journey. Where is it on the map? How long is it realistically going to take? What time will I need to leave? Where should I head for initially? What are my waypoints en route? What will I need to take with me and so on? With some careful thought and a written plan of action, you are more likely to get to where you want to go than if you just tried to drive there 'blind'. Goal-setting is exactly the same. It is not enough simply to write down a goal and do no more. You also have to design a step-by-step action plan that will help you to achieve it.

Say, for example, that a goal of yours is to achieve the full box split stretch. The first thing you would need to do is determine, based on your current level of flexibility, how long a goal such as this should take to achieve. Let's assume it is twelve months. You would therefore write down on a piece of paper the following goal or statement: 'By *the date twelve months from now* I will be able to perform a full box split stretch.' Underneath this you would write 'Action Plan' and detail exactly what needed to be done in order to achieve this goal. For example, you might chose to purchase a book or DVD on achieving the box splits. Be specific though. What book or DVD would you buy? You might decide instead to look on the Internet. This is another good source of information, but detail it on your action plan.

Then you would need to work out a training plan based on the exercises you would need to do and how often you would need to do them. Write it all down so that you commit to it, otherwise you will no doubt forget things, and it will also act as a good motivator when the novelty wears off (which it will). Then you need to pin it somewhere that will enable you to see it on a daily basis. Look at it regularly, absorb what you have written and this will also act as another form of auto-suggestion.

Finally, you need actually to do it. It is no good working out all of this, then not bothering to follow your own plan, or missing the odd day here and there. The reason diets don't work is because people can't stick to them. It takes a certain kind of person who can follow something through to the very end and unfortunately when something takes time to work or develop, we become bored and lose interest. This mentality can actually be traced back to your belief system. The constant dieters who can't resist that slice of cake or bag of chips have not actually conditioned their minds to accept the fact that they are actually going to achieve this goal. Instead, they come up with excuses and justify them by half-heartedly agreeing (with themselves) that they will just have this one, then start the diet again on Monday, as after all it is the weekend.

We all know that smoking will kill us. However, despite all the government health warnings, people still smoke because the endorphin release they receive with each inhalation of nicotine far surpasses their mental clarity that they are actually killing themselves, because it is a slow death – it's not instant. If after every cigarette they were doubled up in agony for thirty minutes, they would soon quit (although I'm sure there are a few who still wouldn't). And yet despite all of this, their mind convinces them to continue smoking in order to satisfy their bodily cravings by having them believe (their belief system once again) that they actually enjoy it. That's how powerful the mind is.

Once you know how to control this, however, you can use it to your advantage and although I'm hoping that everything contained within these pages will help to raise your martial arts to the next level, if just one person who reads this book can take something from this very last chapter and then go on to achieve amazing things with their life it was worth writing – and if you do just happen to win the Lottery after reading this book, then all donations will be gratefully received!

Train hard, keep smiling, live your dreams and appreciate this AMAZING journey we're all on.

Index